THE GLEAMING DARKNESS

CAN YOU FIND THE BEAM OF LIGHT IN THE DARKNESS, THAT CAN BRIGHTEN YOUR FUTURE?

BINA ROY

ISBN 979-888606278-6

Dedicated to my parents, spouse, in-laws, friends, and every person who has made a difference in my life.

I hope this book inspires everyone who is struggling in their life to look at the positive side and identify the beam of light in the darkness.

Contents

"Darkness can teach us many things, including how to improve and excel in everything we do. Its job is to keep everything invisible until we get the first beam of light. Isn't it?"

~ Bina Roy

Acknowledgements

I am highly obliged that you have selected this book.

I have been there in these stories and personally experienced that there are people who do not get everything they deserve in life, but they have made a selfless effort to fight back and find their beam of light even in the Darkness, which helped them change their fortune.

I believe even you can overcome your challenges and experience success if you are determined.

I hope this book will help you develop a positive mindset and take the much-needed step towards self-improvement and living a meaningful life. In short, this book will boost your mind with positivity and remove all the negativity that has been pulling you down.

I want to thank my parents, my in-laws, and my spouse for motivating and encouraging me to follow my dreams. This book wouldn't have been possible without them. Their love and support have made me stronger.

My sincere thanks to the iron lady Dr. Subra Mukherjee - Amazon bestseller Author, and Tony Buzan, Certified Mind Mapping expert, who inspired me to write this book.

My special thanks to Vivek Chaurasia, who shared his valuable inputs and feedback while finalising the book.

They are my inspirations who guided me throughout my writing journey.

My heartfelt thanks and love to all my readers who picked up this book and trusted in me!

And finally, I want to thank the almighty for blessing me with a beautiful life, granting me the opportunity to write this book, and giving me the courage to follow my dreams.

Lots of love, gratitude, and respect,
Bina Roy

Introduction

As a child, I feared 'Darkness' so much that I used to cry for my mother, hoping that she would hold my hand and guide me towards the light. Not very uncommon, right? I am sure even you may have such awful but sweet childhood memories.

But the darkness I am referring to in this book is beyond the literal meaning of darkness we experience in the absence of light. It is more about miserable and unpleasant situations in life, where we feel like being stuck in an endless loop that is dark, and there is no way out. Whensoever we are in the dark and feel alone, even a small beam of light can show us the path to brighten our lives.

Remember, there will be distressing phases in life where you will find people being against you, whether in family, friends, or at the workplace, and they may even force you to give up on everything. Still, it is up to you how you prepare yourself to face them with a positive mindset.

You should learn how to handle every situation instead of complaining about your fate. You need to have self-belief and keep yourself motivated to make all necessary efforts to overcome your challenges and grow in life. Only then will you be successful.

Positivity, affirmation, hard work, mindset, passion, self-motivation, determination, and self-belief are the traits that can help you face any adverse situation in life. If you can't help yourself, no one will. So everything starts with you; you are the one responsible for your success and failure.

I still remember the day in school when my library teacher asked me, "Where is your library book?" to which I replied, "I didn't saw and forgot to bring it."

Even you may be feeling the same thing right now as my library teacher did. "Oh my god, you speak such bad English!" my teacher insulted me in front of other students. The moment when my teacher and the students laughed at me was very humiliating, and I broke down into tears.

Do you think it was a big mistake I made that day?

In life, there will be times when you will feel insulted and discouraged, but it is up to you how you face those insults or handle those discouragements.

Do you learn from such moments and take it as a challenge to prove yourself?

Or do you just sit and cry without doing anything about it and remain the same forever?

Instead of laughing and insulting me, my teacher could have better helped me by correcting where I went wrong. It could have left a positive impact on my mind. Though I was unfortunate that day, I didn't give up. Instead, I made it a point to learn and excel in English, which became my passion and later my core competency and skill.

You may have heard about or may have even experienced workplace politics at some point or the other. Seniors take advantage of the juniors and do not let them grow in life. Their political influence is so strong that even the top management will not allow the junior members to justify their stand and may punish them instead.

Even I have been a prey of workplace politics, which I suffered for quite a long time. But when I had to give up my job due to bad politics at my workplace, I promised myself to prove that I didn't deserve it. Instead, I deserved much better in life.

So, I focused on self-improvement, and with all my dedication and hard work, I kept on achieving small success at each stage that has added tremendous value to what I am today - a Public Speaker, an IELTS Trainer, a Business Communication Coach, an Editor, and now an Author.

My primary purpose in writing this book is to enlighten those who have suffered in life and still sit and cry somewhere in the corner. Remember, struggle is an important part of our life, which teaches us the true meaning of life and gives us the strength to fight back. Without a fight back, we won't succeed. So instead of feeling low, we should be bold enough to face the world by working on our shortcomings and making our weaknesses our strengths.

We human beings can do wonders if we are determined to change our life. If you have programmed yourself to keep thinking about what people will think about me, I am sorry to say, but you have programmed yourself for failure. Trust me, to be progressive, you need to first stop thinking about what others will say, it is only then you will be able to cure the disease called fear, the fear of facing the world.

Many people immediately give up if they are unable to progress as per their expectations; they eventually stop putting effort and then curse others for their shortcomings. Remember one thing; no one can help you unless you help yourself.

The problems and challenges we face in our life are never-ending, so we should not feel discouraged. Instead, we should identify the opportunity to fight and bounce back.

After meeting different people in my life, I realised that those who showed the courage to face challenges have reached great heights and are now shining in life. They have made me believe that nothing is impossible in this world. You can achieve whatever you want in life by bringing in positivity, even in adverse situations.

God has given you this beautiful life, so make good use of it. Make plans, manage your time, and believe that no one can stop you from achieving whatever you want. Avoid negative people in your life, and trust me, whenever you feel stuck and things are not turning out as per your expectation, thank god that he has given you an opportunity to fight back and prove yourself.

If you are alone, you can spend more time on yourself and think about what best you can do for your self-improvement, growth, and success. Even if you don't have enough resources, just focus on the ones you have right now, and you will find a way to make the best use of them.

Darkness is a blessing when you will look and think about it positively. In this book, you will learn about some mind-blowing people and their stories that have inspired me and may inspire you as well.

After reading this book, you will realise that time is precious, and you should not waste it overthinking. Instead, you should take those small steps to improve yourself day by day, which will help you develop the confidence to achieve whatever you want in life.

I hope you will enjoy reading "The Gleaming Darkness" Happy Reading!

CHAPTER ONE

The Gleaming Darkness

Siliguri Central Bus Stand

It was a Sunday noon; the sun was shining bright.

I was eagerly waiting for a bus at the Tenzing Norgay Central Bus Terminus, Siliguri, expecting a friend whom I was supposed to meet after a long time.

I looked up at the clock on the tower, which was showing 12:20 PM.

Aaah, there it arrived, a blue colour Volvo bus, which was as huge as a train coach. I had a dream of traveling on this kind of luxury bus since my childhood but never got a chance.

In a while, I saw a gentleman stepping down from the same Volvo bus carrying a black colour folder in his left hand. The folder contained a few important documents, including my B.Ed. Certificate.

It was my friend Om, who looked quite handsome than the first time I met him during my college days. His attire which included a charcoal grey blazer, navy blue shirt, and black pant, well complemented his looks and enhanced his personality.

"Hey Om, sometimes I don't understand why you always wear these dark colours," I told him instantly.

He gave me a pleasant smile which seemed that he was ok with my comment.

As soon as he handed over the folder to me, I opened it and flipped through the documents to take the first glance of my certificate. "Shreya Roy, B.Ed.," Wow! It was a happy moment for me.

"Thanks, Om. What is your plan?" I asked.

"I have to go back to Purnea, but the next bus is at 2:30 PM," he replied.

We started walking towards the coffee shop to have a cup of coffee and munch on some snacks as we were feeling hungry, while Om's next bus was about 2 hours later.

After entering the café, we occupied the vacant small round table meant for two, with a pair of compact chairs placed on either side.

"Please get us one espresso coffee, a green tea, butter croissant, and a toasted club sandwich," Om passed on the order to the attendant.

I asked him, "How is your family?"

"Better now, trying to come back to the normal," Om replied positively but in a sad tone.

Unfortunately, Om's brother, who was suffering from a bone tumour had recently departed for the heavenly abode at the age of 30. I had even heard that he and his family lost all their savings on the treatment. Now they were trying to come out of the crisis.

To divert the topic I asked him, "Aparna logo se baat hoti hai?" *(Are you in touch with Aparna and all?)*.

"Haan, Kabhi kabhi," *(Yes, sometimes)* replied Om.

We then started talking about the nostalgic moments we had during our college days.

From the very beginning, Om was a little reserved, calm, and composed. Whatever may be the situation, he used to carry a cheerful smile on his face. However, we all knew that he use to often hide his pain under his smile.

Siliguri College...

I remember my first day at Siliguri College; I had caught Om staring at me during our English lecture as if he had a crush on me. His eyes were big, dark in complexion, and he was wearing a loose old t-shirt that was dropping slightly from his shoulder. He was frowning and his face full of questions.

I was annoyed, "I don't understand whether people come to college to study or to have an affair," I told myself.

My thoughts were as typical as that of my grandparents when it came to thinking about the relationship between a boy and a girl.

I often noticed Om in the class, sitting on the corner bench, listening to and observing every student. I thought that maybe he has the habit of staring at people like a vagabond who explore new places and people.

In one of the English lectures, the students were asking questions about English sonnets, a favourite subject of most literature students.

Even I had a few doubts for which I sought clarification from our English lecturer, who was dashing, down to earth, and helpful by nature. The kind of command he had over English was a dream for many. He was so eloquent and proficient.

When I was discussing my doubts with the lecturer, Om was constantly staring at me, which distracted me. "But why is he staring at me?" I asked myself.

After the lecture, I called Om into the corridor, "Hey you, listen to me, and come here."

He came closer, "What is your problem? Why do you stare at me?" I asked in an angry tone.

He gave me a weird look and walked back to the class without any reply. I understood that he had a crush on me and hence could not utter a single word. With an angry look and a red face, even I went back to my class.

In a couple of months, I had made many new friends. Even Om joined our friends' group. College friendship is long-lasting, and yes, we need friends to rely on during our good and bad times. Generally, we make better friends in a few years of college than in 12 years of schooling.

I remember, whenever we had birthdays among our friends' group, we all used to contribute Rs. 100 each to buy gifts and a cake to celebrate. But Om never paid the whole amount saying, "I don't have money; I can give only Rs 10 or Rs 20."

Though we used to accept the amount, it was annoying at times.

"He is so kanjus *(cheapskate)* hai na Aparna?" I said to Aparna.

Aparna, who was my dearest friend, was full of positivity. She replied, "Nahi re aisa nahi hai," *(no, it is not like that)*, but I was very sceptic.

Tusshar was very close to Om; he was the one who always used to spend a chunk of his pocket money on us and helped us in many ways.

Snighda was like a coconut, hard from the outside but soft and cool inside. She used to dislike me during our college days but loves me more now. Sometimes we judge people without understanding them and end up forming a wrong impression.

Arpita, the tallest among all, was so different. She is a darling to all, down-to-earth, no pride, and belongs to a classy family. We all used to admire her as she is a wonderful human being.

Our group was as versatile as unity in diversity. We all were different, had different perspectives but tied in a knot of care and emotion.

The Result!

After the first semester exam, we were astounded by looking at the high marks Om scored when we got the result. We all were bewildered and open-mouthed.

I asked him, "Om, how did you score such good marks? Do you take any coaching?"

He just smiled and replied, "Self-study."

With a strange expression and attitude, Snigdha said, "Natak karta hai, he is a dark horse." (*He acts every time, he is a dark horse.*)

Iwas the one who cried a lot after the results because I gave the exam based on rote learning, which I was not habituated to. I scored lower marks due to rote learning and decided to never do it again.

It is best to understand the concepts thoroughly that will not only help during the exams but also remember them forever in life.

Rote learning is terrible as it can easily paralyse students during exams, not knowing what to write if one forgets a sentence or a paragraph.

Everyone praised Om because of his achievement, and we became his fan. The way he used to explain the concepts to us during our academic years was helpful. Gradually Om became popular among all.

After scoring lower marks in the first semester, we all friends decided to join English coaching.

I told Om, "We are planning to join English coaching; why don't you join us?"

"No Shreya, I can't afford the coaching fee. You all go; I shall manage," he replied with eyes cast down.

We realised that there is something serious in his personal life due to which he denies everything, which involves spending money. I felt pity for him, and since then, there was a curiosity in my mind to find out what Om was hiding from us, and I wanted to know more about him.

Although he often used to say 'yes' to lunch or movies and contributed whatever he could to the bills, he was honest to himself. He never asked or borrowed money from anyone.

One day I asked him, "Oye Om, us din tum mujhe aise kyun dekh rahe thee?" (*Om, why were you staring at me that day?*)

He replied, "I was staring at you so that I could imitate the way you speak English. I am from a Hindi medium school and didn't have an English-speaking environment, and for that reason, I don't have the fluency or confidence to speak as you all do."

I was speechless after hearing Om's reply. I had thought that he was like other boys who like staring at girls. I felt really bad for him and my bad judgement.

My friends started laughing at me; I felt embarrassed at that moment.

A Winter Morning!

It was a beautiful winter morning; we all were basking in the sun after the first English honours lecture.

Our next class was after an hour but got postponed for the day. We were happy as we got good free time to chit-chat with friends and gossip a bit.

Om came straightway from the boys' hostel and sat on the bench nearby. He was carrying a notebook and a few papers in his hands. He looked a bit sad. Suddenly he excused himself and was about to leave the place.

Manisha, the cutest of all in the group, said in Nepali, "Kina gako? Ek chin basihal." *(Why are you going? Sit for a while.)*

I belong to a wonderful place, the queen of hills, 'Darjeeling!' It is the gateway to the North-East, and we can see a mixed culture and religion over here. Nepali, Bengali, Rajbanshi, Bihari, Assamese, Marwari, Buddhists, and people from many other states reside here, though many faces look identical because of the environment.

Similarly, in our group, we all were different in caste, creed, culture, and religion but used to look the same as 'Pahadi.'

Om agreed to Manisha's request and stayed back. He was good at time management; he never wasted his time, whereas we contradicted him in this regard.

Our thinking was 'Coaching me se notes milega, hum woh padh lenege.' *(We will get notes from the coaching centre, we will read that.)*

At that very moment, Om was lost in the papers he had in his hands. I pulled his notebook to see what was there in it, and I was astonished to see that it contained all the English literature notes. I asked him, "Who has given you all these notes?"

He replied gently, "I have prepared it myself."

"Wow! Really?" I responded.

Nilam, very sensitive among all, replied, *"Kya re Om kitna padhte ho, hume bhi sikhao."* (*What Om you are so studious, teach us as well.*)

Om gave a very gentle smile and told, "Yeah, sure."

That day we understood that Om is very hard-working and takes his studies seriously.

Focus on studies is the best option for students from an economically weaker section and a 'no-study-culture' background. It can help them shape their future and change it entirely for good.

The Financial Situation!

A week later, it was Arpita's birthday. We decided to contribute a nominal Rs. 50 each to buy a cake and gift for her. We all gave the amount, but Om did not give anything, saying that I don't have money this time.

Hearing this, Snigdha got irritated and said, "Every time Om does the same thing, he never pays the amount and gives lame excuses."

We all agreed to her point.

At that very moment, Tusshar exclaimed, "No, he is not faking himself. Maybe he does not have even that 50 rupees to pay. Don't worry, I will pay on his behalf."

In the afternoon, when we were celebrating Arpita's birthday in the college canteen with a limited amount and nominal stuff, I noticed a very pleasant smile on Om's face. He was enjoying the moment. Soon after the cake cutting, he reached out and picked a lion's share from the cake and swallowed it.

I was very annoyed and told Aparna and Snigdha, "Paisa toh deta nahi hai but dekho kise itna bada cake ka piece kha liya." (*He never gives money but see how he took the bigger portion of the cake and ate it.)*

Maybe it was my negative side that did not let me understand and apply the true meaning of friendship at the moment. We should never judge a friend based on how much money they have or spend.

Even after the celebration, we girls continued talking about Om and his behaviour during the cake cutting. Tusshar interrupted us and said, "Why are you all discussing all this nonsense? Om is a good guy and genuinely has financial problems."

We decided to end the topic then and there, but I wanted to know more about Om.

The following day we all were sitting in the classroom and discussing about our forthcoming exam. At that very moment, I asked Om, "Om, please tell us about yourself, kaha rahte ho?" *(Where do you live?)*

He replied, "I originally belong to Bihar but live at Dalsingpara near Jaigaon, with my parents and elder brother."

"Where is Jaigaon?" asked Jhilik in a curious tone. She had a dusky complexion but sharp features and was an epitome of beauty. I still admire her.

Many people consider fair skin and look to signify being beautiful, but they do not understand that beauty does not mean only skin colour. The true beauty of a person reflects in their behaviour and how they treat others.

Om replied to Jhilik's Question, "Jaigaon is a lovely place near the Bhutan border."

"Oh, Wow!" I exclaimed, "Have you ever been to Bhutan?"

Om replied, "Yes, it is close to my place, so I have been there a couple of times."

Bhutan is a beautiful country at a time distance of about 4 hours from Siliguri, a very clean and the only carbon-free nation on this planet. It has a friendly relationship with India. You don't need a passport to visit "Phuentsholing" the border city in Bhutan; I visited there once after passing out of college.

We all were so excited to hear this from Om, and there was a curiosity to know more about him.

"And what does your father do?" I asked next.

To which he replied, "My father works in a shop (but did not mention the exact occupation), while my mother is a typical Indian homemaker who accepts everything, whether good or bad calling it a God's wish and our luck. My father works the whole day to take care of our basic needs, which is sometimes not enough."

"So who pays your college fees, and how do you fulfil your other requirements," asked Snigdha.

He replied, "I am here in this college with the help of a scholarship, and I give tuition to students to manage my other requirements."

"Kothai re Om?" *(Where Om?)* asked Jhilik in her sweet Bengali tone.

"Near the college premises, I have a couple of students who are in IXth and Xth grade," he replied.

Hearing his story, we understood that Tusshar was right when he mentioned that Om's financial condition was not good.

I felt so bad that without knowing anything about a person's life, we easily judge them and form a false opinion. I realised that Om's life was full of darkness.

We are so carefree about many things in life and keep on complaining, but Om, despite having a tough life, he never complains. He always carries a confident smile and manages with whatever he has. He is working really hard to fulfil his and his parents' dreams.

We often give less importance to the things we have and worry more about the ones we do not have, but there are people like Om, who are hard-working and have faith that they will achieve something big in life. They do not cry; instead, they seek opportunities to grow in life, and Om was one of them.

The Hostel Room

A few months later, it was the occasion of Saraswati Puja, which is celebrated to pay homage to the goddess of wisdom and knowledge. In Bengal, any festival is celebrated with great enthusiasm and joy.

Saraswati Puja is a popular festival in Bengal, which is celebrated in schools, colleges, and even many homes.

That day girls especially wear yellow saree and enjoy singing and dancing. Many schools and colleges even hold events and competitions to encourage co-curricular activities among students.

Our college too had organised Saraswati Puja, and the entire college, including the boys and girls hostel, was decorated beautifully with the help of a few student volunteers.

Om invited us to see the decoration in the boys' hostel and have the prasad *(holy offering)*. It was the only day when girls were allowed to enter the boys' hostel. The boys too were eager to showcase their hostel rooms in a good state, their way of living and cleanliness, which we all well understood was only for the day, to make a positive impression. The girls were no less either and added exaggerated interjections to their 'only-for-the-day-cleanliness.'

When we all visited the boys' hostel, the hostel in charge gave us the holy offering. Meanwhile, Om insisted we see his room.

In his double sharing room, which contained two compact beds placed adjacent to each other, I noticed a few books piled on the study table kept beside a large window. Spontaneously I asked, "Whose books are these?"

"Mine," Om replied gently.

The books were related to English literature, how to improve English, English to Hindi translation, history of English literature, poems, novels, and a few storybooks.

We all were amazed to see those books because none of us had them, and neither had we ever thought of buying such books.

Arpita said, ''Kya re Om itna padhta hai tu, isliye itna accha marks lata hai." *(Om, you read more that's why you get good marks.)*

Suddenly Snigdha asked a suspicious question to Om "Kha se mila yeh sab books?" *(From where did you get all these books?)*

"I have borrowed them from friends and will return them after reading," Om replied.

Om was serious about his studies and career. While we all wasted our time after the college lectures, Om was busy shaping his career.

It doesn't matter whether you have sufficient money and resources or not but if you have a passion and the zeal to do something big in life, your fate will automatically find its way.

Om was like a deep silent Ocean; the more we go deeper, we will discover something new and interesting. That day, my curiosity and eagerness to know more about him grew stronger.

The Darkness!

After completing our graduation, Arpita, the most intelligent among us, immediately got a government job; while we all were still thinking about what we should be doing next.

Om and I enrolled for M.A., and others planned to enroll next year. The M.A. syllabus was a bit tough, and I found it challenging to manage without any coaching. I was not self-dependent, whereas Om had the habit of studying alone without any help.

Om told me not to worry and he would help me with my studies. Om used to explain to me the important concepts and even clear my doubts about stories, novels, and dramas. Gradually we became good friends, and he sometimes visited my house to teach me. My parents were also highly impressed by Om and his knowledge of English.

In the first year of college, Om was unable to speak English because of which other students made fun of him. But he had completely transformed himself during three years of college. The way Om spoke English now, it was hard to believe that he was from a Hindi medium school.

Even his writing skills were competitive to 'A grade' students from an English medium. English is a universal language, and it is easy to speak if we practice, but writing is a different ball game. We need a different mindset to think and write like an author or a poet.

One day while studying, I asked him, "Om, tell me more about yourself."

He was a bit surprised at the question, "I have already told you all everything about myself and my family, where we live, what they do," he replied.

I responded, "You are from a Hindi medium school; still, your English is so good. You understand every figurative line very well and can explain it so well. Even you are good at English grammar. Whereas I am from an English convent school, but I still sometimes find it difficult to understand the terms. How is it possible? I want to know the secret." *(In an interrogative tone)*

He understood what I meant and added more to his story this time, "Look Shreya, as you know, I originally belong to Bihar due to which I had some Bihari influence while speaking. My father used to repair bicycles, and at the age of seven or eight, even I learnt the repairing skill from my father. My father used to find it difficult to manage everything for my entire family, as his income from repairing bicycles was insufficient, but still, we all managed to live very economically.

I have read about poverty not only in the storybooks but have also experienced it myself as a part of my life. Sometimes, I relate myself to the poverty-ridden, struggling character of Munshi Premchand. We didn't have those luxury appliances at home like a Television, refrigerator, and mixer grinder, but that was ok for us. I was happy with or without them.

The 'no food' days made me think about how to grow, and I found 'education' the only easy and cheap solution to all our issues," this brought a smile on his face and a kind of confidence in his heart.

The best thing about Om was, having nothing was never a problem for him. *Instead of crying, we should think differently and make an effort to change our future for good.*

With a pleasing innocent smile, Om continued, "From the very beginning, I suffered from loneliness and lowliness. I was alone, no one used to value me much, neither did anyone help me in an emotional sense. I have promised myself that I would work hard to achieve something bigger in life."

I understood that Om's life was full of darkness, but this darkness was a blessing for him. Many of us cry over small things, but he preferred working hard instead of crying. Sometimes we think that there is no one with us and we are lonely, but for him, when we are alone, we get more time to think about ourselves, and it can be an opportunity to brush up on our skills.

Om was not like others who fail and give up easily. He was very optimistic about his life. He used his time well and let the positive thoughts and ideas rule his mind even in the darkness.

From the very beginning, Om carried a positive perspective towards everything. At a very young age, he accepted the reality that he had to survive with whatever he had. But he was very sure that he would achieve success in life, no matter what, and knew that he had to work hard for it.

Om mentioned further, "We didn't get much support from our so-called relatives and close ones when we needed them. Instead, they used to mock us thinking that we would always remain the same, but I never bothered about anyone.

Even my neighbours used to speak ill about my family because we were not so well off. We always wanted decent respect in society, which we got for the first time after I topped the Matriculation (Secondary School) examination in my district. The sudden change in people's tone of speaking to us was welcoming for my parents and me. With all these, I have developed a trust in myself that I would achieve success and make my family proud."

If people hate you, never motivate you, leave you alone, it can prove to be a blessing because now you have enough time to improvise yourself. When people demotivate you, you have to motivate yourself.

He said, "I took every opportunity to do something good for myself. There was a 'Moonlight Club' beside my house, and at night the manager kept the keys with us as the club members could visit any time early morning.

I knew the visiting hours of every member, so sometimes when the members visited the club early morning, I accompanied them and used the typewriter kept in the office room to practice. Soon I learnt typing.

Although it is not good to use others' property without permission, that mistake I made during my childhood was good for me. And yes, if the mistake does not hurt anyone financially or emotionally, then it may not be considered wrong.

I used to look for opportunity in every single thing to learn and grow in life because I knew that it is the only way I could do something for myself and my family."

Instead of crying and being upset for superficial things, we should work hard and focus on improving our skills which can help us do something big in life.

Om had a deep passion for English, but he did not get enough guidance to improve his English while in school. He never lost hope and tried to find his beam of light in the darkness.

As quoted by Martin Luther King Jr., *'Only in the darkness you can see the stars.'*

Om was one of the best students in college because of his hard work and dedication. In his life, he faced many challenges, but his never-give-up attitude helped him overcome those challenges and grow in life.

Om mentioned, "I studied in a Hindi medium government school where we never got all the facilities that a private school student could get. In the morning, I used to get up early and help my father repair bicycles before going to school. After school, I used to help my mother to fetch water from the local tube well.

The daily income of my father was very less, so after my studies, I used to also help my brother in binding books, which gave us Rs. 8 to 10 per book and was of little help to the family.

We had to even survive without electricity for five years, but I never lost hope. The darkness encouraged me to fight the challenging situation. When I was in class Xth, I needed electricity to study for my matriculation examination.

My father asked for a bulb connection from our neighbours, but they denied his request. At night, I used to study with the help of 'Kupi' (handmade bottle lamp with a wick).

The low light emerging from the Kupi was less sufficient, so I had to pay full concentration to the subject. As its light was limited only around me and darkness everywhere, there was no reason for me to look or gaze at anything else, so there was no distraction. I used to plan my studies well as I knew that I did not have any other option. The gleaming darkness was indeed a blessing for me."

While narrating this, he was carrying an optimistic and carefree smile. I wondered, how can one be so contented at such a tender age?

Darkness can teach us many things, including how to improve and excel in everything we do. Its job is to keep everything invisible until we get the first beam of light. Isn't it?

The Success!

After getting his M.A. degree, Om immediately got a job in a non-affiliated school in Siliguri, which gave some financial comfort to his family. Even his brother worked in Delhi. We all were very happy for Om and seeing him progress in his career.

But after a few years, his brother passed away due to a bone tumour. While his family lost all hopes, he remained strong to support his family. He lost all his savings on the treatment, and when his brother closed his eyes forever, he was shattered. His struggles were endless, but he very well knew how to handle challenging situations.

He remained firm in every situation, and his 'never-give-up' attitude helped him shine in life. Keeping aside all the negative experiences he had in life, he completed his B.Ed. and kept on working hard on his English and later became a high school English teacher in one of the reputed convent schools in Purnea, Bihar. Om got his affinity in Purnea itself named Deepika, with whom he married in the year 2018 and is leading a luxurious life now.

Many students, teenagers, and people easily give up, but Om is the epitome of success in this modern world and has found his gleam in the darkness. His struggles were not easy, and he worked hard from the beginning, although he knew that his condition was not good. He was focused on changing the chapter of his life and faced every situation with a smile.

Success is driven by one's intent, determination, hard work, consistency, and self-belief. One should focus on these elements to achieve their goals and be successful in life.

Om was very passionate about his education and had a keen interest in learning and excelling in English. Although his primary education was from a Hindi medium school, the way he speaks English and narrates literature is beyond one's imagination. He writes poems and stories, and also gives English coaching to higher secondary students.

While sipping the green tea, I observed him and noticed a few changes in his looks. He looked mature. And the way he handled the attendant and requested for the check (bill) later, was admirable.

I offered to split the bill, but he denied it politely. He was not the same Om the way he was five years back. Paying the bill was a major problem for him then.

"How is your work going on?" I asked him, taking the last sip of the green tea.

"Well enough, I have been appointed as the head of the English Department in school, and I am also running an English institution where I do not just train my students to be good at the subject but also to lead a cheerful life," he replied.

"Wow, Om, that's great! You have completely transformed your life and are making a difference in other's life as well," I said, admiring his achievement.

It was 2:25 PM and time for Om's bus. We bid each other goodbye, and Om headed towards his bus that was approaching the bus stand.

On my way back home, I was continuously thinking about Om and his achievements.

In this world, there are many such inspiring stories and people like Om whom we don't know, but they are an inspiration for many. Om faced many hardships in life but still stood strong and is determined to change many lives by sharing his knowledge and expertise.

Optimistic people try to find their beam of light in the darkness and are determined to eliminate the darkness around them. *Those who dream it can indeed do it with whatever limited resources they have.*

CHAPTER TWO

DISCOVERING MYSELF!

March 2021

Congratulations! And the best speaker of the day is Vaani Roy.

Oh My God! I was so happy to hear the announcement that I suddenly jumped off the chair and hugged my husband in excitement, who was sitting next to me. Even I could see the happiness in his eyes.

It was the first time I stood 'first,' and I could not believe that I had done it. Taking part in virtual speaking competitions was a new thing for me. Still, I kept working hard to improve myself, and finally, the day arrived when I made it.

Looking at my virtual certificate, I repeatedly read the headline, 'Vaani Roy – First Place!' And I knew this was just the beginning.

Immediately within an hour of updating my status on WhatsApp, Instagram, and Facebook, the congratulations and appreciation messages started pouring in. I was so happy to reply with a thank you to each of them, as this was the first time I stood first!

I could not believe my eyes seeing the congratulatory messages even from people with whom I had lost touch; some of them rather used to ignore me earlier. I was feeling really blessed that day.

It was only me who could feel the goosebumps and shivers I got even before I started giving that speech in front of the audience.

Speaking on a stage, whether virtual or physical, the feeling and the amount of tension are the same in both cases. Never in my life had I thought that I would be able to give a speech in front of a larger audience.

I was quite an introvert as a child, but the circumstances changed me completely as I grew up. Even I worked hard and changed myself to prove that I can achieve something big in life one day.

I was truly inspired by the beautiful quote written by Demi Lovato, *'No matter what you are going through, there is always a light at the end of the tunnel.'*

October 2019

I still remember the day when I first entered into 'Taj Ganges' - a Five-star hotel located at Nadesar in Varanasi.

It was my 25th Birthday, so for me, it was a very special evening, which eventuated into a dream come true moment.

Thanks to my husband for making that evening a memorable one for me.

Never before in my life had I stepped into a Five-star hotel.

The red carpet on the cream marble floor, huge chandeliers hanging on the sky-high ceiling, a large vase placed in the center of the lobby, beautiful décor, and luxurious king-size sofa set complemented it with a royal look. "Wow!"

I was amazed!

That day I was completely lost in the beauty of that palace kind of hotel.

I felt like a princess when the darbaan *(gatekeeper)* push-opened the door for me, and the staff at the reception welcomed me with a warm smile.

I started wondering what kind of treatment the real princess used to get when they entered their palace.

A few moments later, we were in the dining hall and occupied the soft dining chair.

Soon after placing the order, two attendants came to serve the food on our table. I was awestruck seeing the beautifully garnished and tempting cuisine being served on our plates.

Suddenly, teardrops started rolling down on my cheeks. Instead of happiness, I was dejected, and my eyes were downcast full of water.

At that moment, the thoughts about my family members living in the village started flashing in my mind.

"They cannot afford to get this kind of food, nor do they get proper two meals in a day,"I whispered to myself.

I was sad thinking that instead of wasting my money *(rather, I would say, my husband's money)*, I could have saved it and given it to them. But I am unnecessarily wasting a huge amount here just to enjoy this evening.

All these thoughts triggered me, and I lost my facial lustre.

"What happened to you?" my husband asked softly, placing his palm on my left hand.

But I did not reply anything; I was in a mute mode.

He understood what was going on in my mind.

He gave me a gentle smile and told me, "We will help them, and we will organise a feast when we visit your village next time."

His words made me feel better, and I enjoyed the dinner with a heavy heart.

God gave me a chance to have an expensive dinner, but I was just lost in my thoughts because I believed that instead of spending money in a luxury hotel, we could save it or rather buy a few days of meals for poor people.

We grow when we help others, and this is the right way to live on this planet by spreading love and happiness. When fate hands us enough wealth, we should help the needy and not waste it.

From the very beginning, I have a soft corner for poor people. In fact, my own maternal uncle and his family are daily wage earners who live in a small hut. My father tried to help them many times in all the best possible ways he could, but even he had his own responsibilities to fulfil.

My father has always been my inspiration, and I can say that I have inherited the habit of helping others from him. He always guides and motivates me to give my best in life, in whatever I do.

I have realised that when you are rich and have money, the people and the society at large respect you, but nobody actually cares for the poor people. This is a bitter truth that many of us often ignore.

Year 2014

I started my career at an early age as a primary school teacher in one of the reputed schools in Darjeeling.

It was almost the mid of the summer season, the first week of May, when my neighbour 'Hema' called me one afternoon. I was just back home after attending the last paper of my final year B.A. examination.

"There is a vacancy in my school; would you like to join?"asked Hema in a firm voice.

I was very excited after hearing about this opportunity and immediately agreed to join. "Yes, I would love to," I replied.

Hema said, "Ok. Then you come along with me to the school tomorrow and meet the headmistress."

"Sure, I will," I accepted her proposal and hung up the phone.

I was still to get my graduation certificate, I didn't have a B.Ed. or M.A. degree, but still, I got an opportunity to teach in that reputed school.

That day I told myself that getting a job is very easy, and my parents nag unnecessarily that nowadays it is difficult to get a good job.

After 15 minutes of informal interview with the headmistress, I got the job, and that too at a decent monthly salary of Rs 7,000/-.

Wow! I was so happy that now I would be independent and can even help my family members.

I always wanted to support my family financially. Since the time I started earning, whatever salary I received, I used to give a small portion of it to my maternal uncle. They were really happy as it meant a lot to them.

My parents were glad to see my kindness, while I was pleased to keep my promise.

Unfortunately, I didn't have a pleasant experience with my first job.

I had completed just three months into the school when a new principal was appointed.

Soon after spending a couple of months under the new principal madam, she started making a fuss over small things wherever I was involved.

Each passing day the new principal made my life difficult by offending and pointing me over every minor fault or error.

I started wondering, is it only happening to me, or others too?

One day she called me to her cabin, "Vaani, you are not able to handle the children, you don't have any past teaching experience, so you will have to leave."

I was shocked! How could she even say me this? While appointing, they knew that I was a fresher, and the school had appointed me willingly.

"Why can't she let me learn and grow instead of demotivating me and insulting me," I started thinking, why? "Did I commit any crime if I am just a fresher? She could have guided me, with love."

I was very disappointed by her behaviour and decided to leave the school after completing that month.

A week before my last day in school, there was an elocution competition, and I was asked to guide the children to form a queue and sit in a row.

All of a sudden, one of the students in my class of grade-1 ran away to drink water, and when he came back, the vice-principal started yelling at me, "Vaani, you can't even handle a small child? Be careful next time."

Suddenly the other senior teacher passed a comment sarcastically, "She is not a mother, so she doesn't know how to handle a child."

I was very upset that day and told my mother about this incident. "Maa, do I have to be a mother first to handle any child in school?"

"No, it is not necessary. Let others say whatever they want to, you don't be sad about it. Just do your work wholeheartedly," my mother replied with a pleasant smile that she always carries on her charming face.

On my last working day at school, the principal told me to write a resignation letter mentioning that, 'I am leaving the school because I am unable to handle the children.'

At first, I denied it, but she forced me to do that saying if you do not write this, we will not give your salary. I was so afraid at that point that I quickly wrote all that she wanted and left her cabin and the school with a heavy heart.

I was absolutely shattered after losing my job. That job was really important for me, but unfortunately, I lost it.

Whatever I may have gone through at that time, I firmly believe that whatever happens, happens for good.

The real intention was not known to me why they manipulated and discouraged me. I was new to teaching, the youngest among those teachers, and they could have helped me learn and grow.

A month later, my neighbour 'Hema' informed me that the school had appointed a lady in my place who is the wife of an army officer.

Although even she did not have a B.Ed., like me, the school's trustee had earlier promised her to give a job. I was just a temporary substitution to fill the gap as the lady was travelling, out station. When she returned, they forced me out and appointed her.

It was a bad experience for me, but I did not lose hope.

As said by Paulo Coelho, '*The secret of life is to fall seven times and to get up eight times.*'

Each time we fail, we realize that those failures are the most significant lessons of life.

No matter how dark the situation may be, finding the ray of light in the darkness and moving ahead can lead us to our destination.

After leaving school, I completed my M.A. and B.Ed., and learnt many new things.

Soon I got another job in an International School, where I worked for four years and gained a good amount of experience in teaching.

I was delighted that now I am all set and doing well in life, I was even helping my family members with my hard-earned money.

But you never know... challenges and difficulties can knock on the door any time in life, so we should be ready to welcome them.

Staying in our comfort zone will not help us grow. If we really want to grow in life, we have to come out of our comfort zone and do something extraordinary.

Year 2019

After marriage, I shifted to Varanasi, a wonderful city in the northern Indian state of Uttar Pradesh.

Varanasi is the spiritual capital of India and is closely associated with thousands of ancient temples and the 88 Ghats on the bank of the holy river Ganges.

After coming to Varanasi, I applied to various schools for the position of English Teacher. I got a positive response from a few good schools, but I always wanted to join a reputed convent school.

Wherever I applied, I was supposed to give an examination and go through the interview process to get appointed as an English teacher.

I cleared the exam in one of the popular convent schools, but I got appointed for the job without any interview.

For a moment, I wondered why they were not following the interview process they were supposed to. I had many doubts and immediately recalled the incident I went through in the first job I got soon after graduation.

There was a conflict in my mind "Am I choosing the right school for myself as I am new to this place?"

But I consoled my mind saying, "Vaani, now you have a B.Ed., M.A., and five years of experience in teaching. So, no one can tell you anything. You are well qualified, have all the capabilities, and yes you will prove yourself."

I accepted the offer letter with a smile and was so contented because this time I would get a handsome monthly salary of Rs 35,000. I can fulfil so many dreams and can help my family members too.

Though my husband works in a reputed company, I always believed in helping my family with my own hard-earned money. Because helping them was my decision and not my husbands'.

On the first day in my new school, I was wearing a yellow saree and was walking very uncomfortably. All the other teachers started noticing me and my discomfort.

When I went to the staff room, one of them asked, "Who are you? I saw you in the morning."

"I am the newly appointed English teacher," I replied.

One of the teachers (Suasan ma'am) interrupted by saying that 'there is no vacancy but......' I was startled after hearing that half-complete sentence.

I told them, "The principal has appointed me for the post of an English teacher."

'Oh really,' exclaimed Suasan ma'am.

They all looked at me suspiciously as if I had made some crime joining here.

I excused myself and straight away went and sat on the empty chair at the corner of the large table placed in the center of the room. I was waiting for the headmistress to allot me some classes.

Soon I got two English classes, and my journey as the English teacher in that convent school began from that day.

I worked wholeheartedly. Even my students liked me and the way I thought.

I met many good colleagues and fellow teachers. One of them even cautioned me about the office politics saying, "Look Vaani, don't share your secrets here; there is too much politics among the teachers, so beware of that."

"Ok, I will take care of it," I replied.

I was wondering, 'Why do people do politics everywhere? Is it really needed?'

I had read somewhere that some people, especially those who are weak enough and have a fear of losing their job or identity, do all kinds of politics to be on the safer side.

Wherever we work, our main motto should be to focus on our work and responsibilities and not to criticise or backbite others.

But I didn't want to engage myself in any kind of politics. I was least bothered.

After a few months, things started changing. The headmistress started observing my activities closely and didn't leave any chance to point out even the slightest mistake she could.

She just wanted to prove that I am not a perfect fit for the school and I cannot do the things that are expected of me.

I was really shocked as if the history was being repeated after five years. The same things were happening with criticism, discouragements, and demotivation.

That day I understood that I was no longer going to stay here. Very soon they will get me out of school. I could feel the negativity in the air.

One day when I was teaching in the class of grade-4, the school coordinator came to me and investigated whether I was teaching independently or taking help from last year's notebook.

After the bell rang, I left the class, but he stayed back to ask a few questions to the children.

The very next day, when I went to the class, one of my students, 'Jhanvi' told me, "Ma'am, Shashtri sir was asking about you and how you teach? He asked whether you use any guidebook or not, do you sit in the class or not, ma'am, why was he asking all these questions?"

It was really disappointing, but I replied to Jhanvi, "He was asking all these only to know your requirements."

This kind of close observation and investigation continued for almost a month, and they realised that everything was ok with me and the students remained quiet and happy in my class. There was no scope to raise any negative points about me.

Still, one day the headmistress called me to her room and said, "Vaani, you are not performing well. What kind of English do you speak? The students don't understand your high-level English and the way you teach, and they even complain about you."

Her words dumbfounded me because I always use to take the initiative to help the children and clear their doubts. She told me that the parents also complain about me because I do not teach well.

I replied, "I am new to your school, so please guide me the way you do to help new teachers learn and improve."

Different schools have different ways of dealing with things. But instead of guiding me or showing me the way to do better, she started blaming and demotivating me.

I understood that it is not my fault but they really don't want me now. There is something fishy, and they have some other plans.

I understood that they just intended to appoint good teachers for a few months as a substitution when the old permanent teachers went on a long leave.

Even in the past, a couple of new teachers were asked to leave the school after a few months. They can't say directly that we do not need you anymore, so they make all kinds of excuses to remove the teachers appointed just as a temporary substitution in the absence of their permanent teachers.

From that day onwards, the headmistress started pointing at me unnecessarily and sometimes blamed me in front of the other teachers.

I slowly started losing the confidence I had gained in the past five years.

Do you think a teacher who is an M.A. and B.Ed., can't teach or handle a class of the primary section?

All of us are different! We are human beings; we do make mistakes, but holding someone's hand to help them and guide them can really do wonders in their life.

When I realised that they were planning to remove me, I started working harder and also proved myself in most areas, including curricular.

All my students were happy with me, including their parents. I got good feedback from them, but I don't know why the headmistress used to pass those negative comments. She never appreciated me for all my hard work and good performance.

One day when I was explaining a story in my class of grade-3, all the students were quietly listening to my words. Suddenly, a large monkey gate-crashed from the window and came inside the classroom. All the students jumped from their seats as they saw the monkey and started screaming out of panic.

Within a few minutes, the teachers in the nearby classrooms came to the rescue and helped me manage the situation.

It is quite obvious that when you are engaged deeply in something and if any wild animal appears suddenly in between, then naturally the panic and scream will be our primary reaction.

I was called for an explanation of the situation to the principal's cabin.

"When a teacher was there in the class, how could all the children scream so loud? You are so careless and don't know how to control the class," the principal asked in an angry tone.

I listened to her calmly, with self-questioning thoughts popping in my mind, 'What did I do? Am I responsible for the monkey in the classroom?'

When any such incident occurs unexpectedly, we need at least a couple of minutes to control the situation. We teachers are also human beings. I know it was not my fault; still, the principal found a chance to point out and scold me.

I thought that it was ok. Maybe it was my fault, as I couldn't handle the situation well. I should listen to her and follow her instructions so that I do not face any problems in the near future.

The Year 2020

A drastic change came in my life when I lost my job during the Covid-19 pandemic.

It was a lockdown, and I was taking the school classes online.

In the middle of the class, I got a call from the principal, "Vaani, you will have to leave the school as we can't afford to pay the salaries."

Hearing this, I felt numb and couldn't utter a word for a few seconds.

"Hello Vaani, are you there?" asked the principal in a screeching voice from the other side.

I gathered some courage and requested, "Please let me continue. This job is really important for me and my family."

"Isn't your husband working? Tell me first," she asked rudely.

"Yes, he is working, but what is the connection between his and my job. We both are self-independent, and yes, one should be," I replied to the principal, clearing my stand.

"Don't be so selfish Vaani, I can't pay you. Sorry!" the principal passed on her final decision.

The word 'Selfish' really broke me down. After that, I could not speak a single word and just said "OK" before disconnecting the call.

Since the time I started my career, I had been demotivated by many of my colleagues in the previous schools where I worked.

They considered me timid and even took undue advantage of me whenever they could. And with a smile on my face, I used to do everything for them. Not just because I was timid or foolish, but because of my humbleness.

We should never change our humble nature in any circumstances because that is what we are!

I faced a lot of challenges during my academic as well as professional life because I was an average student and a less experienced English teacher.

Although I gained much more experience in life, I was still weak in terms of practically handling a difficult situation.

Many a time when I was unable to complete my task properly, instead of help and guidance I used to get scolded and was even insulted in front of all.

Nobody motivated me, but still, I tried to be strong because life is a journey, and there will be many ups and downs.

We can handle difficult situations and even come out of them with flying colours only if we dare to face them strongly.

After losing my job during the pandemic, I felt devastated and helpless because it was a phase where we were in a complete lockdown. It was tough to find a new job in a situation where many corporates, organisations, and schools had stopped fresh hiring's.

The worries and thoughts were constantly swirling in my mind. 'How am I going to help my family members now?'

Looking at my condition, my husband tried to console me and told me, "I will help them, you don't worry, I will pay."

"No! They are my responsibility, not yours. You don't need to do this," I replied in an angry tone.

As it was my responsibility to send the money to my family every month, I could not tell them that I had lost my job. Instead, I tried to help them with the bit of savings

I had because it was a promise I had made to them and myself.

My maternal uncle once asked me, "How is your job going on? Are you getting enough salary?"

With a smile on my face, I replied to him, "Yes, I do have enough money, you all don't worry."

The lockdown phase was so miserable for the daily wage earners that they had no work. So, looking at the situation, I continued to help them without letting them know about my present condition.

It took me almost a week to come out from that trauma of losing a job. I was disappointed thinking that the principal and the headmistress could have guided me wherever I was going wrong. But they didn't want to guide or motivate me because they had their plans beforehand, whom to appoint and whom to remove.

I understood everything that transpired that day because I had been through a similar situation back in 2014. I understood their intentions and their way of selecting and later getting rid of temporary teachers within a short period.

But this does not mean that they are not good to others or are bad human beings. They are good and even guide others, but they were professionals in the end. They knew what was in their best interest at the moment, and accordingly, they kept adding or removing as per their needs.

I am not blaming anyone for what I went through but rather encouraging you to always prepare yourself for the worst.

If no one supports you, you better support yourself. Come out from your comfort zone to achieve great heights and prepare for it.

Soon I decided to work on improving myself, keep myself occupied, and promised that I am not going to waste my precious time anymore. I will utilize my time productively to sharpen my skills. I will prove to everyone that 'challenges will keep coming in life but keeping yourself strong in every situation and handling them with a positive mindset is the key to success.

Many people called me only to know how I was and what I was doing after losing my job. But no one called me to extend their help or understand my situation.

Soon I started making educative videos to express myself on virtual and online platforms.

I remember the day when I first thought of creating my own YouTube channel. I had heard that we need resources like a professional camera, tripod, ring light, good background or backdrop, good mike, good content, and good clothes to create good YouTube videos. But we actually don't need all of that.

What is needed the most is the courage and skill to speak with confidence while facing the camera. You need to have a passion for changing yourself and improving a little every single day.

We always wait for positive results but still leave the task we choose midway instead of being consistent. Consistency requires patience, hard work, faith, and a call to action.

I learned that, whatever you want in life, you can get it only if you are consistent enough. Consistency is the key to achieving any goal, and yes, to reach the goal efficiently, we should always focus on the process. We should also track our progress, what we are doing and how?

I remember the first video I recorded and posted on my YouTube channel. Some people criticised me, commented on the quality of my content, the way I speak, grammatical errors, and many other negative comments. But still, many others tried to encourage me with positive feedback.

You will get all kinds of people in life. Wasting your time thinking about the 1% of people who would hate you or criticize you is useless. Instead, you should focus on the other 99% of people who would love you, help you, and guide you.

I came across many people who just tried to mock me. I could even sense the feeling of jealousy they carried for me. I thought that all my near and dear ones would support me, but there were many even among my relatives and known ones who were not happy, or rather I would say they didn't like to see my progress. No one called me and said that 'you are doing well, and these are the areas where you can improve upon.'

I was all alone finding my ways but never hesitated to seek help from people close to me and guidance from some experienced people I met on virtual platforms.

That day, I understood that if you want something in life, keep trying and track your progress. Never over-expect anything from anyone. When people do not talk to you or leave you alone, it means you have an opportunity and ample time to groom yourself.

Do not waste your time on gossip and unwanted activities that can affect your efficiency. Avoid attending unnecessary parties and functions to get quality time to improve yourself, stay away from all the negative talks that can kill your wisdom and time. Instead, invest your time to challenge yourself.

I met a few good people through online virtual platforms who helped me understand my worth. Every day I worked on improving and grooming myself and gaining knowledge, with a positive thought to rise again.

Remember if no one motivates you, you will have to motivate yourself because it is you who knows yourself better than anyone else in the world.

My journey to becoming a public speaker began in December 2020. I learnt many things with the help of my mentors, and yes, they really motivated me.

Public speaking platforms have really helped me learn more and improve myself. I participated in various public speaking competitions but was unable to win. Still, I continued to participate in speech contests without worrying about the results.

Soon I became a good speaker; although I was not up to the mark, self-motivation and dedication helped me a lot.

With continuous hard work and efforts, I have reached a position where I am now an English trainer, a business communication coach, a public speaker, and a content creator. All this was possible only because of my consistency, self-motivation, and positive mindset.

I always dreamt that I would be holding the trophy, securing the first position one day. Although I worked really hard, I always doubted my abilities, as I lacked the much-needed self-belief and self-motivation.

But since the day I started motivating myself by saying 'Yes, I can achieve what I want in life,' I had started gaining confidence, leaving all the negative thoughts behind. I found myself gradually climbing the stairs of success.

Looking into the best speaker certificate, I realised that consistency, affirmation, hard work, and a positive mindset can change our entire life.

We always cry for the things we don't have in life. But we never look at the things and resources which we have.

Twists and turns are a part of life, so taking every single criticism as a blessing can change our life. Criticism boasts us to correct and grow ourselves.

A few months later, I got a call from the principal of the convent school. She said, "Vaani, I saw your videos on YouTube; you are really doing good."

I replied, "Thank you, ma'am; all this was possible only because of you."

"God bless you!" the principal ma'am exclaimed.

Holding the certificate, I dropped a few tears on it. Those were the tears of happiness, a reward for my accomplishment, and the promise that I will always be a lifelong learner!

CHAPTER THREE

LIFE IS GOOD

"Sometimes it is our destiny which defines our life, but more or less it is how we accept our destiny and then try to find ways to add beauty to our life. We cannot just sit back and cry about what God has given us; rather, we should accept whatever the situation may be and then find a meaningful purpose and ways to build our destiny. Whatever comes in our way, we can take it positively and accept it with good grace."

A Morning in Darjeeling

It was lovely weather in Darjeeling.

The rising sun was peeping out on top of the Kangchenjunga Mountain range, spreading its golden rays on the beautiful tea gardens.

I was sitting on a couch on my balcony, reading a book about emotional intelligence.

As I was spending my leisure time, I could hear the whisper of the wind, complemented by the tune of birds who were busy singing their early morning song.

The cool breeze softly smoothed the whisp of my curled hair onto my cheeks, which I tucked gently behind my ears.

While I was feeling the beauty of nature, unexpectedly, I got a call from my Mentor, Ms. Ashmitaa Singh.

She is a beautiful soul who always guides me in learning the values of life apart from English enhancement.

"Hello Trisha, how are you?" asked Ashmitaa ma'am in her soft tone.

"I am good; what about you ma'am?" I replied.

"Same here! Listen, I want to tell you something. Recently I have joined the IELTS English course, and I have learned a lot and gained so much knowledge. Even I want you to join this course, as it will benefit you in future," said Ashmitaa ma'am.

"Oh really! What is the course fee?" I enquired.

"Well, now there is a 30% discount on the course fee. I will text you the number of the institute, and you may please call and talk to the counsellor. You can give them my reference," she replied.

"Thank you so much, ma'am!" I was overwhelmed hearing about the new opportunity for learning and self-improvement.

"Most welcome, Trisha," responded Ashmitaa ma'am, before ending the call.

That day I was so happy that I would be on my new learning venture and soon take my English to the next level.

As I always wanted to become an English trainer, I quickly dialled the number she had texted me and spoke to the counsellor.

Without delay, I enrolled in the course; and even texted a thank you message to Ashmitaa ma'am letting her know about the enrolment.

Meanwhile, I was thinking about Ashmitaa ma'am, a teacher by profession; she is an educator, trainer, coach, public speaker, podcaster, orator, YouTuber, and fashion stylist expert.

Oh my god!

Just at the age of 45, she has accumulated so much knowledge and talent.

She may be wealthy and may have two or three home helps to take care of the house.

I was truly inspired by her because at an early age she is well settled, happy, financially stable, and has gained wisdom.

She has achieved everything in her life and can live her life happily.

Wow! So lucky and blessed she is. I told myself.

I saw her daughter in one of her videos; she is indeed beautiful and charming like her mother.

Her family looks classy, but by the way, I haven't seen any pic of her husband with her in any of the posts on her Facebook page.

Maybe he is very busy with his work, or perhaps I could not find their picture on Facebook.

I was first introduced to Ashmitaa ma'am through an online public speaking platform, where the members practise public speaking and communication skills.

I had never met her in person, but still, we feel so close and connected. Thanks to the virtual meeting platforms and other social networking apps.

Although she is based miles away from the city where I reside, we have developed such a close relationship that we never felt the barrier of distance.

A month later, I called Ashmitaa ma'am to update her about my development on IELTS.

During the call, Ashmitaa ma'am told me, "Hey Trisha, let's meet next Saturday in Delhi; what do you say? Some of our public speaking club members are planning to meet over lunch in Delhi. Why don't you join us?"

"I can't say anything right now as I am busy with my IELTS course. But I will let you know soon," I replied, as Delhi was far a distance for me.

"Ok. I understand. I will wait for a positive reply," she said before we disconnected the call.

Until late at night, I was thinking about what I should do. It was a golden opportunity to meet such a magnanimous lady.

With some hesitation, I spoke to my husband about it, and without any second thought, he responded, "You should visit Delhi and meet Ashmitaa ma'am."

I was delighted!

That very moment I picked up my phone to book my tickets and even dropped a WhatsApp message to my IELTS trainer that I would be traveling over the weekend and won't be available for the IELTS class.

On Saturday, I took a morning flight to Delhi to meet her.

I was very excited as it was supposed to be our first meeting in person. There was also a curiosity in me to know more about Ashmitaa ma'am, her family, her husband, her life, how she takes care of herself.

Undoubtedly I wanted to be multi-talented like her, and I even admired the way she carries herself.

Meeting in 'The Grand - New Delhi'

I reached 'The Grand - New Delhi' a premium hotel located in Vasant Kunj, New Delhi, where we were supposed to meet over lunch.

As the hotel was close to the Delhi Airport, I reached earlier than expected.

Dressed in formal attire for the occasion and with a smile on my face, I sat on the large couch placed in the center of the lobby, waiting eagerly for Ashmitaa ma'am to arrive.

After a few minutes, I saw a beautiful lady who looked much younger than her age coming towards me.

She was wearing a pink floral print gown with matching sandals, whereas her earrings complemented the pink shade of her lipstick.

She looks so gorgeous! I admired her.

It was as if a dream come true moment for me. The lady who always guided me is standing in front of me today. The feeling was beyond my imagination.

"Hi Trisha, How are you?" she asked with a gentle smile.

"I am good ma'am," I replied.

She hugged me before we occupied the couch again.

We complemented each other and started talking about the activities we were presently doing to shape our skills, talent, and career.

I was constantly praising her wisdom, knowledge, style, and the way she carries herself.

She is an epitome of a multi-talented woman, managing her career, life, and family so well.

Suddenly, I expressed my happiness, "Wow! Your husband is so good, and he supports you a lot. You are so lucky that you can manage your family along with focusing on your career."

Surprisingly she remained tight-lipped and avoided talking on the topic. She instead preferred discussing IELTS.

I thought maybe she unknowingly changed the topic.

But, after a couple of minutes, when I asked her, "What does sir do?" she replied hesitantly, "He is at home; he does nothing."

I was a bit shocked and quiet for a few seconds and was blaming myself for asking such needless questions.

A curiosity arose in my mind because whenever we used to speak on the call, she used to say that her husband was not at home.

She always avoided any conversation related to her family life for some reason. But why?

I understood that she was hiding something, and she would never talk about it.

Meanwhile, I was telling her about the hardships I faced during the Covid-19 lockdown. I had lost my job and suffered a lot during that phase, and somehow I managed to enroll in the IELTS course.

"Trisha, you are young, and whatever you are doing right now will be beneficial for you in the future. So, dream big, stay positive, and enjoy the journey. You will shine one day," she consoled me.

Hearing those words, I felt encouraged and realised that Ashmitaa ma'am has a lot to tell.

Without wasting much time, I asked, "Ma'am, I would like to know more about your life. How do you handle and manage your family and personal life?"

"You are working, have two children at home but are still able to focus on different courses and effectively doing all by yourself. How? I want to know the secret," I urged her to tell.

Ashmitaa ma'am agreed and began narrating her story to me...

"Look Trisha, we always judge peoples' life looking at their appearance, the outfits they wear, especially in their posts on Instagram, Facebook, and the pictures they share on WhatsApp status. But there is always the other side of the coin which we do not see.

Everybody has a story in their life, and looking at their Instagram and Facebook posts, we easily form a perception that the person is happy and lucky enough. We feel delighted and aspire to get the same. But the truth could be different than what we actually see."

The Flashback - Meerut

"I was born in Meerut and did my schooling at Sophia Girls School. My father was a successful businessman. We had a wonderful life in the beginning. We were rich, had a huge property, money, and reputation.

But soon, my father lost everything because my uncle cheated on him and got our business and the property transferred to his name.

I had a terrible childhood as we struggled a lot when my father lost everything, and he had to rely entirely on my uncle, even for his petty expenses.

My father wanted to take some action against my uncle but could not do so, as he had no money. He was also not ready to accept what had transpired in his life.

He could have taken some action, but he felt helpless as there was no one to support him.

He was unable to face all the pain and hardship my family was going through after my uncle snatched his business and the property.

He was under tremendous pressure and tension as he could not fight back for his family and soon gave up, ending his life at an early age," Ashmitaa ma'am said, with her eyes moist.

She continued, "Life is a precious gift to us from God! We should be thankful for it, and we have no right to misuse it under any circumstances. We must have the intention, courage, and strength to face our problems and come out from them.

But it was the opposite in my father's case who decided to depart from this world, leaving us and all his responsibilities behind.

My mother somehow managed both the children, but still, she had to depend on my uncle for money.

She knew that everything belonged to her husband; the business, the money, and the house were hers, but she couldn't get a single penny without my uncle's permission. He was very dominating.

We were utterly dependent on my uncle, who sometimes used to torture our family with mental harassment so that we leave the house and move to my grandfathers' house.

You know Trisha, I had to go through the pain and suffering at a small age and observed everything that happened to my family.

I was helpless but at the same time, I had many dreams in my eyes. My life changed after my father passed away, and I suffered the pains but fought at the end to get back my life."

'If the problems in our life seem never-ending, we should not feel discouraged; rather, we should be thankful for the opportunity to fight and bounce back.'

"I promised myself to change my life in a way, 'the caterpillar struggles to break the shell and come out of the cocoon to transform into a beautiful and fly freely.'

I knew that I have to struggle, but I was determined to change my life.

From the very beginning, I was submissive and always felt proud of my nature, my humbleness, I am strong, but now I feel that why didn't I speak up and take action for the sake of my family. Why did I tolerate every single torture and harassment?

When I was in school, I had many dreams in my eyes. I was a bright student and never missed an opportunity to learn and grow.

When we were staying in my grandfather's house, a man who was almost double my age used to come to teach my brother and me. I used to see him as my teacher and guide, and when I turned 18, I got a marriage proposal from him.

Despite not knowing much about marriage and him, I accepted the proposal. I thought he would take care of my family's responsibilities as no one was there to look after my family.

There was no objection from my mother because of her helplessness.

When I got married, it was in my mind that I would finally get a family from whom I would get love and respect. But destiny had some other plans for me."

'We can polish ourselves and shine in life only when we face each of our problems and challenges with a positive mindset. We just need to be strong and hold our patience.'

"I was very innocent and wanted to pursue higher education. But getting married at an early age changed my life completely.

The person with whom I got married was not good as a human. He used to beat me, mock me, and sometimes even torture me. I was completely shocked and helpless.

I was being treated as a maid by my husband's family. They used to mock me and had complexities because though I belonged to a wealthy family, now we were left with nothing. They always tried to control my life.

Before my marriage, I didn't realise that this person was not earning well. Without knowing anything about him, I took the most crucial decision of my life and spoiled my precious years.

After a year, my in-laws forced me to give birth to a child. Though I was mentally not prepared for it, I gave birth to a beautiful girl. For me, that day was a beginning of a new life.

But my husband's family was not at all happy, and they abused me because I gave birth to a girl child."

"Ladki paida kiya hai, iska kharcha kaun dega?" *(You have given birth to a girl, who will pay for her expenses?)* my mother-in-law said.

"I sat crying at one corner carrying my daughter in my arms, wiping the tears on my face, while my husband was smiling and making faces, supporting his mothers' comments.

The mental harassment increased day by day, and they crossed all the limits. Still, I was submissive, believing that this was my family and I had to go through it because it is my destiny," she said in a painful tone.

I could feel her pain and emotion while Ashmitaa ma'am was narrating what she went through.

Holding back her tears that had started peeping through her eyes, she strengthened her tone and said, "I kept myself strong because I knew that I have to now live for my daughter. I never wanted my daughter to go through all the ups and downs I faced in life. So every night I used to study.

Moreover, I even wanted to support my mother, who still had the responsibility of my brother.

One day, my mother went to my Uncle's house to ask for financial help as my brother was suffering from cancer.

But my uncle denied saying, 'I have already spent a lot on you and your children, now I don't have anything for you. You can go from here and never come back.'

My mother pleaded, but he didn't show any mercy on the pity lady.

A few months later, my brother passed away after losing the battle against cancer.

My uncle and my in-laws had crossed all limits, but still, I was submissive; there was no other place for me to go.

I cried out loud for my only brother. I could not believe that God had taken away earlier my father and now my brother at an early age."

An hour passed, but the other members of our public speaking club had still not arrived. Only we two were there as we decided to meet a little early before the planned time for lunch, and I got a chance to listen to Ashmitaa ma'am's story.

While narrating her story, tears rolled down her eyes. I felt guilty because she was so happy to meet me, but I reopened her old wounds by asking about her family life.

The Grand - New Delhi

"Sorry Ashmitaa ma'am, I asked you the wrong question at the wrong time," I apologised.

She smiled and hugged me and said, "Thank you, Trisha. Today I am feeling good because people always say that I am blessed and lucky, but they don't know what I have gone through in life."

Our faces grew pale but she was feeling relaxed after sharing her bitter life story.

'Even your bitter life experiences can help you unleash your energy to bounce back strongly and bring the real you.'

"Hope everything is fine at home. If you are facing any problem, do let me know," Ashmitaa ma'am continued the conversation.

I replied in affirmation, nodding my head as a gesture, as I was still keen to know about her bounce-back story.

"Ma'am, you have been through a lot. Tell me, how did you manage to improve the situation," I asked.

To which Ashmitaa ma'am unveiled the other part of her story...

Flashback to Meerut!

"The physical and economic harassment continued for a couple of years. One day I was forced to leave the house, and when I denied they beat me up. The next day they locked me in a room without food and water, and my daughter was also not given food.

This way, many years passed with domestic violence, suffering, harassment, torture, but I never took any severe step against them.

I had given birth to my second child, and it was a boy this time.

My teaching career started when I applied for a Teacher's post in a Government school, and I got the job.

My in-laws, including my husband, were happy, not because I got the job, but because now I will fill their pockets with my salary.

This time I thought that everything would be fine as I had delivered a boy child, got a Government job, and could also provide money to the family.

But less did I know that the struggle in my life was still to continue. Whenever I received the salary, my husband used to ask for it, and if I denied then the whole day, I had to remain without food and water.

I had the job, but still, I didn't dare to speak against my husband and in-laws because of my submissive nature.

Although I feel proud that I was tolerant enough to give multiple chances to my husband and my in-laws, I scold myself for being too submissive.

I regret it now because I allowed all this to happen to me.

I could have fought back initially, but I remained quiet and suffered a lot because I considered that it was my fate and they were my family members. No matter what, I will always be with them.

But remember one thing, there's a limit to one's tolerance. Maybe my limit was a little more than any other normal human being of today's generation.

In October 2015, it was my daughter's 10th birthday; I was so happy and brought a cake to celebrate her milestone of completing a decade.

I called a few of her friends to celebrate the occasion. My in-laws were against that event as they believed that wasting money on a daughter's birthday was a wastage of money.

But that day, I took the first step to say no, though in a fearful voice, for my daughter's happiness.

My daughter was dressed in a pink coloured fairy frock and was looking like a princess. Both my children were waiting for their friends to join in.

But it seems my mother-in-law had decided to spoil the occasion. She came and warned me to stop all this."

"Stop this birthday celebration," my mother-in-law shouted in a firm voice.

"We will finish the program within an hour; please, I beg of you, do not hurt my child today. It is her birthday," I responded.

"But my mother-in-law became furious and immediately called my husband to get home soon.

A few minutes later, my daughter's friends joined us to celebrate the event, but the entire scene changed when my husband reached home. He was drunk as usual."

"Stop this party," he shouted out loud in a nasty tone and flung the cake in the air.

"All our happiness and celebration went in vain, and the other children just panicked and ran out of the house, leaving their gift packs behind."

"Why did you do this? It is your daughter's Birthday," I retorted.

"Don't argue with me," my husband replied and landed a tight slap on my face without any reason. He even shouted to both the children.

"If that was not enough, my husband and in-laws exploited me and my children and threw us out of the house.

The whole night I was standing and begging to let us in. I was a teacher now and was even wondering what people would think. Without worrying too much, my husband closed the doors.

It was the day when I lost my tolerance and thought of taking action. But soon, I fainted on the ground. Looking at the condition, one of my neighbours immediately reported to my husband. In a panic, my husband brought us inside the house.

To cover his shameful act, he called my mother and provoked her. He complained that 'your daughter is characterless' and whatnot.

My mother tensed and called me early morning at 4 AM to know about what had all happened."

I explained to her all the incidents that transpired the last night, to which my mother responded, "leave the house, Ashmitaa. I am there to take care; we will manage somehow."

"That day, I decided to leave the house and even file a divorce against my husband to end our relationship. I could feel the relief and took a deep breath.

Meanwhile, my husband was sorry for his actions and tried to convince me not to leave the house.

You see, Trisha, the time had changed, and now it was my turn to be in power. I realised that I am powerful, educated, a qualified teacher, earning well, and I am the queen, not a slave.

For so many years, I had been allowing them to torture me, and I had understood that I was the queen of my life.

These many years I was just struggling to break the shell of the cocoon to come out, and now I am a beautiful butterfly ready to move wherever I want."

I was touched listing to Ashmitaa ma'am's bounce-back story.

'Whatever you go through in life, you can become an inspiration to others by sharing your bounce-back stories.'

Tears rolled down my cheeks after hearing her story. I couldn't control my emotions, and I hugged her tightly and kissed her cheeks.

"You are a powerful woman, ma'am. Love you and more power to you."

She was so happy and relaxed after telling her story.

"Listen, Trisha, always believe in yourself and remember one thing you are not a slave, and nobody has the right to judge you.

I still live with my husband, but that is my own house, and I purchased it with my hard-earned money. My relationship with my husband is not good enough, he is still the same, but now I have learned to say no. Even he knows that I am much more powerful. I don't respect him anymore, but I have allowed him to stay in 'My house' because of my values.

I have decided to live a wonderful life, and now I am free like a beautiful butterfly, and I know my life is going to be the best. Because I am capable of making all the decisions in my life, nobody can say anything. I don't want people to pity me as I am strong. And I am happy with my supportive children.

A small gesture can change your life anytime, so always love yourself, know your values, and always believe in yourself."

Those words really inspired me, and I realised we easily give up. This is a big shout out to all those who are still suffering and just dragging their problems.

'Never stop loving or believing in yourself. Defining your values and understanding the true meaning of life can help you come out from the darkness and give a new direction to your life.'

I was feeling blessed as Ashmitaa ma'am came early to spend some time with me, and I was able to hear her inspiring story.

Meeting other Members 'The Grand – New Delhi'

Soon the other members of our public speaking club started arriving, as per the scheduled time.

We all greeted each other and started discussing about the kind of videos we make to improve our communication. This virtual platform had united all like-minded individuals who wanted to transform their lives.

I know, all of us have some or other challenges and struggle in our lives. Instead of running away, we should face them with pride. 'Struggles play a crucial role in shaping our life.'

I was carefully observing the other members and noticed that they all were smiling and rejoicing at the moment, but they too had stories inside them. They too, have struggled in their life, but it is really difficult to judge anyone by looking at their faces.

After a wonderful meeting and an awesome lunch, we bid goodbye to each other.

We all left with beautiful memories, but I left full of learnings and with a wonderful story of a caterpillar who struggled hard to break the shell of her dark cocoon and finally transformed into a beautiful butterfly, spreading happiness and love to all.

CHAPTER FOUR

THE AWAKENING

An Evening in Varanasi

It was a rainy September evening, and was drizzling outside.

I was busy in the kitchen when suddenly my cell phone started ringing.

'Who is it now?' I quickly washed my hand and rushed towards the drawing-room to grab my phone.

It was my husband Siddharth on the other side.

"Yes Sid, tell me," I said, accepting the call.

"Hey Anisha, what are you doing?" asked Sid, over the phone.

"Nothing, just busy with cooking. What time will you leave from office?" I responded, shooting back another question as it was already past 7 PM.

"I am occupied with some urgent work right now, and it will take almost 2 hours to wind up. Ok, listen," said Sid, his voice excited, "I called to tell you that Prakash will be visiting us tomorrow evening."

"Oh! Wow. I haven't met him before," I replied.

"He is expected to be in Varanasi tomorrow for some personal work. So, I invited him for dinner. Hope that's fine with you?" Sid continued.

"Oh Yes, it's absolutely fine. Be back soon," I hang up the call, smiling.

Prakash was Sid's friend whom he met on a flight during an official trip to Delhi, last year and was impressed by him as they shared some common interests. Since then, they have been in touch and have become good friends. Sid makes it a point to meet him over drinks and dinner whenever he is in Delhi.

Hosting the Dinner

The next day, since the afternoon, I was busy with dinner preparations.

At around 7:45 PM, Sid's car arrived and stopped near the main compound gate. I was standing near the front side balcony and saw a gentleman getting down from the front passenger door. He was of average height, dark complexion, wearing blue jeans and a white T-shirt, carrying a small backpack.

I understood it was Prakash; I was waiting for them for quite some time and had kept everything ready.

I opened the main door before Sid could reach out for the doorbell.

"Welcome, Prakash Bhaiya *(brother)*," I greeted, inviting him inside.

"Hello Bhabhi *(sister-in-law)*, it's good to see you," Prakash replied, with a smile, and handed over a small gift pack saying, "This is for you."

"Thank you so much," I responded, accepting the pack.

"Please be seated and feel comfortable," Sid told Prakash, signalling his right hand towards the sofa.

"Wow, nice home. It looks big. In Delhi, we will have to pay a big rent to get such a huge space," Prakash said, trying to be as mellow as possible.

"Yes, the houses in Varanasi are big and beautiful, and the best part is that the rent is affordable," said Sid.

In the meantime, I had headed towards the Kitchen to get the tray of fritters, snacks, and water.

"What will you have? Tea or Coffee?" I asked Prakash.

"I would prefer a cup of tea," he replied, looking towards Sid, silently enquiring if he has the other preference.

"Anisha, tea for me too," responded Sid.

"Cool, you guys carry on. I will be back in a while," I replied and headed back towards the kitchen.

While I was preparing the tea, I heard an unfamiliar ringtone. It was Prakash's phone ringing. He accepted the call and was having a conversation with the other person in English.

Prakash seemed to have good fluency in English and a fair accent, which sounded quite natural.

I couldn't help overhearing the conversation as he was loud and clear on the call, which ended in a couple of minutes. I understood that he was talking about the delivery of a project, which may be related to his work. Sid had once mentioned that Prakash works in one of the top IT companies.

The tea was ready, and I was back from the Kitchen with 3 cups of tea and placed them on the centre table.

I handed over the cups to Prakash and Sid before lifting my cup and sitting on the couch placed adjacent to the sofa.

"So, tell me Prakash Bhaiya. How is it in Varanasi? Hope you liked the city," I interrupted their previous conversation.

"Yes, I really like this city. It is my second visit to Varanasi. I was here almost five years back, and now I am seeing a huge development in infrastructure with the new highway, flyovers, and better road connectivity. It has changed completely," he replied, sipping the tea.

"Even we have heard about the development and experienced huge changes in the last two years since the time we have been living in this city," said Sid, agreeing to Prakash's statement.

"So, what made you visit this city today?" I enquired.

Prakash laughed and said, "Well, I am almost 30 now and think it's the time for me to settle down, so I am looking for my perfect match as a life partner. I was here to meet a girl and her family."

"Oh! You should have told us before; we could have accompanied you," I said, moving my eyeballs quickly towards Sid.

"Yes, you should have," Sid seconded my statement.

"Well, I would have loved to. But it was a sort of a private meeting," he said. "To be honest, I don't like this system of seeing girls and interviewing them for the marriage purpose, but it was my father's command this time to meet the girl and her family, which I couldn't deny."

"Ok. I guess we could have helped make your decision easier," I replied.

"Nothing sort of decision from my side. I would be happier if the girl's family liked me and finalised. I don't want to keep on meeting girls," Prakash said in a bit-tired tone.

"But why would anyone deny you. You are well settled, have a good job, what else do they want?" asked Sid.

"My friend, as you know, there is a huge caste-based system which is a drawback but still dominant in our society," Prakash responded. "I belong to a Scheduled Caste, so I have already faced many rejections in the past."

"What crap! How does it matter if the boy has good qualities?" I retorted, completely disagreeing with the caste-based system.

"Yes Bhabhi, but not everyone thinks in the same way. I gave my best today, even liked the girl, but her family belongs to a caste higher than mine, and I could sense that they were not very comfortable after learning about my caste," replied Prakash.

"Koi baat nahi, iss se acchi mil jayegi," *(no worries, you will get much better)* said Sid in a confident tone.

"But Prakash Bhaiya, you are well qualified and successful; shouldn't it count?" I asked.

"Hmm, I can call myself a bit successful in my professional career. I am working as a senior project manager with an MNC IT company and have a good package too, but I don't have any professional degree like an Engineering or an MBA," replied Prakash.

"I somehow managed to complete my graduation and hold a diploma from a private computer institute that has helped me with software development skills and reap the benefits for my career," he continued.

"These professional degrees are just a piece of paper that gives you a tag. I have seen many degree holders who are not good at their work. What truly matters is the experience, and I am damn sure that you are well qualified for the Project Managers position; otherwise, you wouldn't have reached there," said Sid.

"Yes. True," I agreed to what Sid said.

I could sense that Prakash had gone through a lot, which we don't know, and I was curious to hear his story.

"So, Prakash Bhaiya, what stopped you from pursuing a professional degree? I want to know," I started bombarding my questions to get a new exciting story. Now I realise how mean I am.

"Well Bhabhi, I don't like to think and cry about my past, but since you asked," Prakash cautioned me before starting his story, and his statement clearly stated the pain he had hidden within.

Flashback Story – Maihar, M.P.

"I originally belong to a small town called Maihar, which is located near Satna, Madhya Pradesh."

"Oh really, you are from Maihar? We have heard a lot about Maa Maihar Devi Temple, located on a hill-top but never had a chance to visit," I said in an exciting, followed by a disappointing tone.

"Yes, it is one of the popular holy places in India. The temple on top of the hill is beautiful and gives good peace of mind to the devotees," replied Prakash, "though I spent my childhood in this town, it was not an ideal one as any child would want."

"I am the eldest son in my family and have two younger siblings - a brother and a sister. My mother passed away early in the year 1999 due to Tuberculosis.

I was only 7 then and didn't understand much, but I still have some vague memories about my mother, how my siblings and I used to play with her, how she used to feed us and sing cradle songs to make us sleep at night," said Prakash, and his eyes moistened.

"After her death, my father was worried about how he would take care of his three children. After all, he was a poor farmer who worked the whole day on the field to earn and feed the family."

"My grandfather and relatives suggested he gets married again and get a new mother for us.

Though the intention of my father and grandfather was right, as a child, I found it difficult to accept our new mother at first. I initially hesitated to be with her or call her maa, and it took almost a year to be comfortable with her. It was much easier for my siblings, who were just 5 and 3 years old at that time.

During the day when my father used to be out for work, I spent more time with my grandfather as he was the only familiar elder face I had in my family.

My new mother was kind and tried to give us the motherly love we wanted as a child. Slowly and gradually, I lost the memories of my mother and started living in reality," narrated Prakash, and my eyes were filled with tears, listening to his childhood loss.

He continued further, "As I turned 10, I understood that my father needed someone to help him in his agricultural fieldwork, so after returning from school, I used to reach the field to help him. Though he used to ask me to go back home, I wouldn't listen and was very stubborn in this matter. I think I grew up at an early age.

I studied in the village panchayat school, where the teachers were less punctual, and I took my primary education till Vth grade in Hindi. My father couldn't afford the high fees of the only English medium convent school we had in town.

After passing the Vth grade, I got admission to the secondary school where we were introduced to the English language and started learning ABC and later English words and sentences. I found it interesting to learn a new language. I had heard this language a few times before and was even familiar with the alphabets as I had seen them on billboards carrying English language, but couldn't understand anything," he smiled.

"Wow, the way you speak English now, it is hard to believe that you started late," I replied, recalling the conversation he was having on the phone some time back.

Dinner Table Conversation

I looked at the wall clock and realised it was already past 9 PM.

"It's past 9 PM. Should we have dinner? It is ready," I asked both of them.

"Yes," came the reply, both Prakash and Sid echoing together.

As I was serving the dinner at the dining table, "Wow, the dishes look delicious and tempting. I can't wait to start," said Prakash.

"Thank you Bhaiya, please start," I was glad to hear the compliment.

Taking the first bite of chapati with the fish curry, Prakash asked me, "Bhabhi, even you are an English teacher, so you would understand the importance of English very well."

"Yes, I do. English is a universal language that has a huge impact on our growth and success. And this is one language that everyone should learn, or else it will be difficult to succeed in our career," I replied, smiling.

"Right! Thankfully I understood the importance of English at an early age. Once I started learning this language, I started teaching it to my brother and sister simultaneously, who were still in the Hindi medium primary section. Indeed, I wanted them to learn this language early and be good at it.

My habit of teaching this language to my siblings helped me excel in English, and I developed a good command of the language by the time I was in class Xth," said Prakash, considering it as an achievement.

He continued, "Though my father and new mother looked after us, I loved my grandfather more and was closer to him. He took good care of us and greatly influenced me, and shaped me into what I am today as a human being.

He was very knowledgeable and used the verses of the Bhagwad Gita to teach me good things and how to succeed in whatever I do. I still apply those verses whenever I am in a dilemma, and even refer to the Bhagwad Gita to find the solution to my problems."

"Wow, Prakash, I wasn't aware of your interest and knowledge of the Bhagwad Gita," Sid said, raising his eyebrows.

Prakash smiled, "Yes brother, it is a comprehensive book one should read at least once to transform their life."

I was impressed with what he said and decided to read the Bhagwad Gita, next.

"So, how did you get into I.T.?" I asked.

"That is a separate story; you would find it interesting," replied Prakash, smiling as if he understood my intention of capturing his life story.

"Do you know what is the biggest challenge for the school kids in small towns and villages?" asked Prakash, feeding a big spoon of biryani in his mouth.

Some thoughts popped up in my mind, but I wasn't very sure about what he was referring to. So I just shrugged my shoulder and waited for him to give us a hint.

Prakash said, "The biggest problem is lack of quality education and not getting easy access to the latest technology. Village schools are still lagging, and many of them do not have a single computer and cannot offer computer education or access to it.

The Passion for Learning, But the Financial Dilemma!

My first encounter with the computer happened in my junior college, which set up a small computer lab with just 6 computers for over 300 students. For me, it was a new thing altogether, though I had seen it before in the SBI Bank branch of my village. I was excited to learn how to use it and found it fascinating."

"Yes, you are right. Even I come from Siliguri, a small town near Darjeeling. But I think there we as students had better access to technology than many other villages," I said.

"Hmm. But Anisha, many villages are still way behind and need a big improvement in providing quality education," said Sid.

"Right. When I got access to a computer, I was curious to learn more about it. I used to spend more time in the computer lab whenever it was vacant. While the computer teacher was available for a limited period, I took the help of the computer lab in-charge to clear my doubts as even he had a fair amount of knowledge.

One day I asked him about making a career in computers. I had heard that people with a computer background earn more. He told me that there is a massive demand for software developers, and I can consider doing a software development course soon after completing my XIIth. I imprinted this on my mind that I want to learn more and excel in this," Prakash continued.

"Even before I could complete my XIIth, I had started enquiring about software development courses. Unfortunately, the course wasn't available in my town Maihar, but there were some computer training institutes in Satna, almost 50 Km from my place. I had decided that I will learn it even if I have to travel miles.

One day I went to Satna to get complete details about the course. But when I heard the fees, I was shocked. They demanded about Rs 50,000/- for a 2-year part-time diploma course, an amount I had never seen in my life together," Prakash said, with a little smile on his face.

"When I spoke to my father about the course and mentioned the fees, he denied the idea straight away and told me 'kyon yeh computer diploma ke chakkar mein pad rahe ho, apna college khatam karo aur koi acchi sarkaari naukri ki koshis karo' (*why are you getting into a computer diploma, focus on completing your graduation first and try for a good government job*).

Initially, I was furious hearing this but later realised that my father was a small farmer who didn't have enough savings and had to even think about my siblings and the family. I calmed myself down.

I think *anger is our biggest enemy and of no use. It blocks the mind and stops us from making the right decision. One should instead learn tolerance and self-belief as it gives the strength to face even the biggest challenges in life.*

I had a few sleepless nights thinking about letting go of my dreams. I would have preferred waiting instead of backing out completely.

Later my grandfather suggested we borrow some money from the zamindar (*landlord*) by mortgaging the small piece of land he had. I was a bit hesitant, but he trusted in my capabilities.

Soon my grandfather mortgaged his land and managed to arrange the money for the fees.

I enrolled for the course and opted for an evening batch (6 to 9 PM), though my father was not very happy about mortgaging the land," his eyes reflected the pain of disappointing his father.

You may not always get the resources to achieve your goals, so do not cry for or regret not having enough money. You can change your fortune only if you want and are ready to give your 100%.

"I started working hard. Every day I had to attend my college in the morning, manage the fieldwork in the afternoon, and travel 50 Km by public transport to attend the course in the evening, reaching back home by 11 PM. Sometimes I broke physically, but I was mentally strong and determined and never gave up. I kept my patience for two years, as I knew it would be rewarding in the long term," continued Prakash.

This reminded me of a beautiful quote by Dalai Lama, 'Tolerance and patience should not be read as signs of weakness. They are signs of strength.'

"Wow, Prakash Bhaiya, you are amazing," I appreciated his effort and hard work.

"Yes, Anisha is right. You are truly amazing," said Sid, emphasising my words.

We were done with the dinner and having the desserts.

"Thanks, but my true struggle had not yet begun," said Prakash. My eyebrows raised after hearing this, and I was curious to know about the struggle.

"Maihar was not the best place to build a career in software development, as there were no I.T. companies or any I.T. related job in the town then.

I had two choices, either find a job and move to a bigger city or start something of my own. Starting my own business required huge funding, which was out of the question. So, I started hunting for a job as the computer institute couldn't get me a good job which was promised initially," Prakash expressed his disappointment.

"So, did you get the job immediately?" I asked, unable to control my curiosity.

Prakash smiled, "No. It was past six months, and I had no job. What I realised was that there was no opportunity for freshers and that too if you are only a diploma holder without any engineering kind of degree.

My plans went for a toss, and I had the pressure to earn money and get back the land mortgaged with the zamindar.

The zamindar was like a hawk sitting on the prey and was looking to confiscate the land if we failed to repay the principal amount on time. We had already paid huge interest on the loan, and now it was time to release the land.

My grandfather requested him to give us a year time to repay the debt, and he agreed after long deliberation.

I had to listen to my father's harsh words almost every day, as I was unable to get a job with decent pay. I felt helpless and was feeling sad for my grandfather who believed in my capabilities, but he never complained and always told me never to lose hope."

"Oh, I can understand your pain and situation," said Sid, placing his left palm on Prakash's forearm.

Prakash continued, "The luck struck, and I came across a small proprietorship firm in Satna, who were looking to digitalise their business.

They were looking for candidates with an I.T. background, and I got the job on a contractual basis, which means I will be jobless again once the project is completed and the contract is over.

I thought, at least something is better than nothing, and this was the opportunity for me to gain some experience."

As said by Catherine Pulsifer, *'To see an opportunity we must be open to all thoughts.'*

"In this first job of mine, I had to hear a lot from the owner. He was very arrogant and harsh to his employees and often used slang words. Working with him was humiliating but I had no option of moving out until the project was completed.

I worked hard and completed the project before time in one year with an additional six months of the maintenance period.

With the money I earned in this job, we managed to repay the debt and release my grandfather's land. And the experience of a year and a half was decent enough to land me a good job. I was not a fresher anymore," Prakash said, smiling.

"So, this time, you got the right job...." I said.

He continued, "Yes, based on my knowledge and experience of delivering a project, I got the opportunity in a mid-sized I.T. company in Bhopal as a junior level software developer at decent pay.

But, that was not enough. I was just 23 then and had many dreams and responsibilities too. I had to shape the future of my siblings and give them the best.

I had moved to a new city, which was much bigger and more developed than my town. Though I was earning reasonably well, I had to spend like a miser, as I had to send money home.

My focus was clear that I need to grow in my career. I gave my best at work and got good appreciation and ratings from my managers and promotion too."

As quoted by Theodore Roosevelt, *'Believe you can and you are halfway there.'*

"You may have worked really hard for this success. I am inspired," said Sid, smiling.

"Thanks, brother," Prakash responded and continued further, making himself comfortable on the sofa.

"Things were going well. Everything seemed to be under control when my grandfather's health started deteriorating.

He was over 65 and had developed some heart-related ailments. He had to even go through angiography, and we had to spend a good amount on his medical treatment, which was manageable with my pay."

"Oh! I hope he recovers soon. And what about your parents?" I asked.

"I now have a better relationship with my father and my mother. My father sometimes regrets the wrong opinion he had about my diploma course. He now understands the importance of this course that has not only helped me fulfil my dreams but also improve the lifestyle of my family.

We have built a bigger house now. My siblings are doing well with their studies. I manage to pay their fees on time and always encouraged them to take up some professional courses. I don't want them to struggle the way I did.

My sister has recently completed her LLB and is considering an LLM, while my brother is doing a B.Tech."

"Wow, you have done really well and achieved so much in a short time and lesser age," I said, wondering how one can achieve so much at a tender age. He is not even 30 now.

Time is precious, which once lost is lost forever; you may never get it back. So you should make the best use of your time to learn and gain knowledge and enhance your wisdom, and make all efforts to achieve your goals within a set time.

"Yes, I had no choice but to work hard to grow and be successful in my career. Backing out of my goals and responsibilities was not an option for me.

The Paradigm Shift

I did well and even learnt a lot in those three years while working for the I.T. company in Bhopal. But the paradigm shift in my career happened after one of the recruiters approached me for a role of a project manager in a Delhi-based MNC.

I knew this was a life-changing opportunity for me, so I prepared well before heading to Delhi for an interview. The interview went well, and I was selected out of 15 other candidates for the role. Probably, my knowledge and experience over other candidates may have helped me get the job.

This boosted my confidence, and I haven't looked back since then.

I have been working with this company for over two years and have been promoted to senior project manager last year. I would say that I have grown with the company."

If you chase money, money will act dear and expensive. But if you chase knowledge & wisdom, money will follow you and be with you as a friend forever.

"Wow!" I exclaimed, feeling happy and proud of him.

"You have really transformed your and your family's life. I am sure that your parents and grandfather will be proud of you and your achievements.

For someone who didn't have the privilege of getting the best education and other facilities but still managed to reach a higher position and leading a team is a big thing," said Sid, winking at him.

"Yes, it is, if you are determined and focused on achieving your goals," Prakash responded with a smile.

Bidding Goodbye

While talking, we didn't realise the time. It was past 10:30 PM.

"It's too late, and I think I should leave," Prakash said, looking at his wristwatch.

"Why don't you stay here tonight? You can leave tomorrow morning," Sid suggested.

"Yes, please," I requested.

"I would have loved to spend more time with you both, but I have an early morning flight to Delhi, and before that, I will have to check out from the hotel by 5 a.m. I promise I will plan it better next time," Prakash replied.

"Wait, we have something for you," I said and headed towards the room to get a gift pack.

"Please accept this," said Sid, passing the pack to Prakash.

"What is this for?" Prakash questioned.

"Just a small token of today's meeting," I replied, smiling.

"Thank you so much. I will remember this day forever. I have never received such love and affection from anyone before," Prakash said, and his eyes were moist, "I had come to this city today to meet my would-be life partner and will be going back with memories of a new family."

"That's so sweet of you. I am sure you will get your life partner soon and that too of your choice where you don't have to compromise because of your caste. Just have patience; good things take time. And now that we are a family, even I will start searching for a nice girl for you," I said, encouraging him.

That was an emotional moment for me and Sid as well. "Come, let's have a selfie," Sid, raising his mobile phone with his front camera ready to click a couple of pics.

"Wait, I will drop you at the hotel," said Sid.

"Yes, please," replied Prakash, picking up his backpack and the gift box.

"It was nice meeting you, Prakash Bhaiya. See you again soon," I said, bidding him goodbye.

"Thank you, Bhabhi, for the lovely dinner. It was my pleasure meeting you," said Prakash before leaving, with Sid following him out of the door.

I was feeling great to meet a personality like Prakash.

While cleaning the dining table, the memories of our meeting and discussion kept flashing through my mind.

"What a person he is. No wonder why Sid keeps on talking about him so much," I told myself.

The meeting with Prakash was awakening. I understood that money is not everything in life; it can help fulfil your needs but not necessarily give you self-satisfaction. It can help you get a degree but not gain knowledge and wisdom, which you will get only through your self-determination and quest to learn more.

It is rightly said that '*You can do anything. You can be anything you want to be. As long as you believe in yourself and work hard.*'

CHAPTER FIVE

THE SILENT MESSAGE

My Final Day in Varanasi

The Sun was shining bright!

I just passed through the garden area of our home and stood near the gate, watching how my husband was trying to fit the luggage in the boot of the Car.

I told him, "Could you please load my flower pots."

"No Kiran, there is limited space in the car so, leave all the pots behind," replied Parth.

I requested him again, but he was firm and not ready to load them.

I was feeling sad, not because of those flower pots but because it was finally the time to leave the city where I spent almost three crucial years of my life.

I remember, when we initially shifted to Varanasi in 2018, I used to tell my husband, 'I don't want to stay here in this unknown place.'

But now, when it's time to say adieu, I was feeling bad. Somehow I was trying to control my emotions.

Down the stairs in the kitchen, our landlord aunty was busy deep frying some puri's for us. She had already cooked chole, and litti-chokha, favourite cuisines in Uttar Pradesh.

The love that the landlord aunty gave us during our years in Varanasi was beyond imagination, and she always treated me like her daughter.

She packed all the food items in a bag and told me, "Raaste me kha lena." *(Eat on the way.)*

Feeling her love for us, I was filled with sad emotions and couldn't hold back the droplets of tears that started rolling down my eyes.

I replied in a soft voice, "Aunti, aap ne khane mein itna kuch banaya hai." *(You have prepared so many dishes.)*

Yes Kiran, all these are your favourites, so I thought to make it for you the last time, as I don't know when you will visit us again.

My tears were about to roll down again, but somehow I controlled them by bringing a smile to my face and touching her feet to take the blessings.

Bidding everyone goodbye, we left the place.

We were supposed to drive from Varanasi to Siliguri (my hometown) and later to Guwahati, as my husband had got a new job and was posted to a new city in the northeast state of Assam.

Leaving Varanasi was very painful for me as I was there for almost three years and gathered many memories.

My love and devotion for Lord Shiva increased here as I learned more about Lord Shiva by regularly visiting the Kashi Vishwanath Temple and interacting with his devotees out there.

It is really a beautiful place to live in.

I felt emotional and was about to cry in the car while crossing the Malviya Bridge situated on the river Ganga.

The distance between Varanasi to Siliguri was about 800 km, and we were sure that we would have to take a halt somewhere in between.

Even our parents clearly instructed us not to drive at high speed, stay in some hotel at night, and continue our journey the next day.

The Night at Darbhanga, Bihar

To reach Siliguri, we had to cross the state of Bihar. The roads in Bihar were still not up to the mark; they were narrow, had uneven road surfaces, and contained numerous potholes.

It was almost dark after the sunset, and after 9 hours of drive, we were about to reach Darbhanga, a city situated in the Mithila region of Bihar.

We were double-minded about whether we should continue driving at night or take a halt in a Hotel.

"Call Suraj," Parth told me, his eyes were glued on the road while driving.

Suraj was our old neighbour in Varanasi, who belonged to Darbhanga. But it was more than a year since he got posted to Delhi.

I unlocked my phone, scrolled through my contact list to locate his number, and tapped the call button.

"Hello, Suraj Bhaiya, How are you?" *(in a bit confused tone, wondering whether he will recognise me or not)*

"I am good. What about you?" *(he shouted out of excitement)*

In the meanwhile, I put my phone on speaker mode.

"Bhaiya, actually, we are driving to Siliguri and are about to reach Darbhanga. Could you please tell us whether it is safe to travel at night from Darbhanga to Siliguri?" I asked.

"The road is good, but I would suggest you both do not travel at night. Rather why don't you both stay in my home?

I will call my brother Poorabh to escort you both," replied Suraj.

"No, Suraj, we don't want to trouble your family; we will stay in a hotel. Please tell us where I can get a good hotel to stay in," answered Parth.

Suraj requested, "No, please, I request you both not to stay in a hotel as my home is nearby, so please visit my home. I will tell my brother Poorabh to send you the location and co-ordinate with you."

We could not deny his request.

In a couple of minutes, a WhatsApp message notification flashed on my screen. It was from an unknown number.

Poorabh had shared his home location so that we could reach the exact location, and in return, I shared our live location with his number.

Following the location on google maps, we entered a village where there were hardly two street lamps. The lanes were dark and narrow, covered with bushes on either side, and we could see small huts and a few concrete houses.

While passing through the lane accompanying the field, I saw something unexpected. Still, women in the smaller villages go for a wee outside in the field.

I was surprised because already many developments have taken place in the country after 75 years of independence. However, looking at them, I felt bad and wondered why the condition in rural areas is still the same.

Ignoring everything, we reached the location shared by Poorabh.

Suraj's home was a mid-sized single-story house surrounded by a waist-length boundary wall and a small iron gate.

As soon as we halted our car in front of the gate, and got down we were welcomed by Poorabh who escorted us inside and even held our luggage.

His parents were happy to see us, as they were smiling but did not say anything.

Suraj's mother hugged me tightly and used sign language to communicate with me. She even held my hand, took me to her room, and made me feel at home.

At first, I was confused, but within a minute I understood that she cannot speak and even cannot hear.

I felt bad about it; my heart melted and brought tears to my eyes. At the same time, I was a bit confused as I had no idea how I should respond to her gestures.

"You are so lean like my daughter-in-law and very sweet," Suraj's mother expressed in her sign language.

I was confused and looked at Poorabh, who was smiling and 'Nodded, Yeah.'

"When will you have a baby?" she asked in her sign language.

Poorabh *(with some hesitation)* tried to explain to me what his mother was saying, and in return, used sign language to explain to his mother what I replied.

This was the first time I understood that you don't really need words or a language to communicate; love and expression can be more than enough.

If you have love in your heart, you can make others feel happy and comfortable with your expressions and can even convey what you mean.

A few minutes later, when I asked his father about his well-being, even he used sign language to express his thoughts.

I was totally in trauma and was surprised to see both husband and wife being deaf-mute. When I asked Poorabh, he told me that both his mother and father could not speak and hear.

I started thinking about how it was possible. It was hard to believe that both of them have such disabilities, while they have three healthy and beautiful children who are well educated and established in their careers.

I whispered to myself, "Wow! I am so lucky to meet an amazing couple who, despite being deaf-mute have raised their three children and are happy."

There may be many sacrifices, struggles, hard work, torture, and even teasing hidden behind their happiness.

When Suraj's mother was cooking, I tried to help her, but she repeatedly used her sign language to tell me, "You, please sit and relax."

But then, because of curiosity, I continuously stood beside her to notice her expressions and actions, the way she replies, and how she calls her son.

Meanwhile, my husband Parth was sitting beside Suraj's father, who was showing him the designs and some handicraft work they had created.

Even he stated in sign language that 'we are very happy that you both visited here.'

Both husband and wife were carrying a pleasant smile on their face, and they were so happy to adore us.

In eagerness, I couldn't stop myself from asking Poorabh a few questions. Although I hesitated a bit, my intention was not to hurt anyone's emotion or sentiments.

"When Suraj bhaiya, Neha didi, and you were children, how did you all manage with your parents? I want to know. They must have faced many problems and challenges to raise you three, Right?" I asked.

"Yes, from the very beginning, Maa and Papa faced challenges and hardships. We three were very small at that time," replied Poorabh.

He further continued, "My Naani *(grandmother)* once told me that when Maa was only 16, since that time, she used to get many marriage proposals. But as soon as they were told that she was 'deaf-mute,' they withdrew their proposals and were not ready to accept her. Soon Maa got her kind of match and married the one who was similarly a deaf-mute."

"People used to make fun of them and used to call them Bhera and Gunga (deaf and dumb). Both even cried tears of blood, but they never gave up on them and not even on us. Especially in the village, people are less educated, and they commonly use slang words to communicate if they find any problem in the other person. They considered being deaf-mute is a sin."

I understood that, in a small village, you would get respect, love, fresh air, and people will whole-heartedly welcome you, but many of them will still have narrow mindsets and thoughts because of a lack of awareness. Such malpractices can be seen in most of the villages.

"This is really not done, and I think this is because of the lack of education and facility in the village, as I have seen women and men still go outdoors for a wee. Even if you make them understand, they will ignore you, and some of them may also stand against you. They are simple, but there should be someone to remove the blindfold tied on their eyes," I said.

"Yes, you are right! Still, there are many people in the village, who call us the son of Bhera and Gunga," replied Poorabh.

He continued, "My parents suffered humiliation and teasing by the village people. For my Papa, self-respect was everything, but he never got the kind of respect he deserved, neither from anyone nor his family; people used to disrespect both of them. They both thought that if they worked hard and earned some money, maybe they could live a respectable life, but even then, no one valued them or gave them a job. Somehow they used to manage their livelihood and feed us. They got some help from my uncle, but he soon stopped helping them as he too, was poor and could not manage with his own family.

My Papa somehow managed to open a small general store, but he could hardly sell his goods, as there was no one to help him. People used to avoid visiting his shop, thinking that he would not understand as he could not hear and speak.

As the family grew, there was too much pressure on Papa to satisfy our needs. He made some plans to attract customers through audiotape and started playing the audio about the things we sell in the shop. Gradually, customers started visiting the shop."

Suraj's mother understood what we were talking about. She came near to me, and in sign language, tried expressing how she faced challenges while raising her three children.

She expressed, "Nowadays people, especially the young generation, don't want to work hard or accept challenges. They give up easily.

Despite being deaf-mute and facing all the humiliations, we both raised three children. It is not about people; it is up to us how we show the courage to face all the challenges and change our life.

Yes, people will say different things to you, but in that case, you should avoid them as you cannot make them happy every time."

When I looked at her face and her expressions, I touched her feet, saying that you both are the epitome of inspiration and we should learn from you.

Many of us give up very easily when we realise that a certain task is difficult. Although we even promise ourselves in the beginning that we will accomplish it, but most of us give up in between and never try again, and then we cry about our failure and inability.

What I believe is that *life is a hurdle race with many ups and downs; they will be with us forever. Our success depends on how we dodge and cross those hurdles and keep moving ahead.*

We should make our weaknesses our strengths, and with a consistent effort, we can overcome any problem or challenge.

God has blessed us with all the capabilities, but we still sit and cry. Just think about this old couple; despite being deaf-mute, they have not only set an example in front of their children but have even proved to the world that your deficiencies cannot be a hurdle if you have the will to face the challenges.

People may not like you or help you, but if your near and dear ones are supportive, then consider yourself among the luckiest ones on the planet. You don't have to worry about anyone.

Poorabh was feeling good sharing his pain with us, "I heard many stories from my Naani, and whenever she used to describe my parent's journey, Maa used to cry and used sign language to give her consent. Although we did not get enough materialistic things, we were happy with whatever little we had in our small home.

My Papa was a small shopkeeper; due to lack of money, he couldn't do anything extraordinary for us, but he promised himself that he would get back his self-respect and will have a bright future for his children. He kept himself strong, maybe because he could not get proper education during his childhood, but he was determined to have a wonderful life for us."

"My Naana-Naani (grandparents) helped a lot in our upbringing; although they were not able to help us financially, they helped my mother by taking care of us when we were kids.

When Suraj bhaiya was born, my entire family was tense about whether he will be able to hear and speak or not. My Naani used to sing in front of him when he was an infant to check his hearing capabilities.

Initially, Suraj bhaiya did not respond, but gradually he started responding to every action done by my Naani," continued Poorabh and later explained the same to his mother in sign language.

Suraj's mother *(interrupted using her sign language)* "Yes, Poorabh is Right!" *(she snatched the words out from Poorabh's mouth and started making sign gestures to speak)*

"I remember the day when my elder son called me 'Maa' for the first time. Though I was unfortunate that I couldn't hear his words, for me it was as if I got my voice." *(Crying impatiently and feeling blessed)*

In the words of Alice Howes, *'We both trying to find our own inspiration and movement. My inspiration was sign language.'*

She continued stating the story in sign language, and Poorabh translated it to us.

"I remembered when my elder son was just six years old, and we took him to an English medium school to get admission. The school principal asked my child a few questions, and he responded well, but when he asked us, we used sign language to respond. Immediately the principal rejected him and told us, sorry, we can't give admission to your son because even the parents have to clear the interview.

We requested by joining our hands, but he didn't agree. I was cursing God; what have we done. Despite being poor, we thought to get him admitted to a good English medium school so that he could grow in his life, but because of our disabilities, even our children had to face rejection.

My elder son did his education from a government school and used to get the first position in his school, and even topped the state board in his class XIIth. We two were helpless to help him, but he was very mature from an early age and used to study by himself.

After two years, I gave birth to a daughter. When she was born, I was so scared because I very well knew how difficult it was for a girl to survive in a village if she is deaf-mute. I used to continuously check with her, but my daughter turned out to be beautiful and has no flaws in her, by God's grace. She is very pretty.

Nobody used to play with my children, as other parents didn't allow their children to play with them. The families with an orthodox mindset used to hate us and considered us unholy for the village as if we had done a crime being deaf-mute. Life seemed to be like hell at that time; I used to cry and be worried about what would happen next.

Both the children used to go to school and faced loneliness until they were in class 10. They were very supportive and mature; they never took any ill-action by the villagers to their heart. We know that if God takes away one thing, he gives something else in return. Only we need to be strong in the storm. After my daughter, I gave birth to my youngest son 'Poorabh' who was very aggressive from the beginning. He never used to tolerate any foul words against his brother and sister, and not even for his parents."

While translating this part of her sign language, Poorabh smiled at me and said, "We can't tolerate the torture every time, and sometimes we need to speak up for ourselves and, more importantly, for our self-respect. My parents cannot hear or speak, but we three were there to break the stereotype."

Suraj's mother nodded and continued expressing, "We even faced suppression. A wealthy villager deceived the only small piece of land we had by defrauding us. When we produced the property documents, even the police rejected them, saying it was forged, and labelled us liars.

My husband and I fought together, but no one stood in favour of us. My family was uneducated, and even they were unaware of anything. We lost the only asset which we had kept for our children. That night we cried a lot, but the next morning brought a new day, a new beginning. We both promised to stand for our rights and fight against injustice. Although we were deaf-mute, God has given us eyes and hands."

In life, we cry and complain about the things we don't have; instead, we should look for what we have and how we can use them for our good.

She stated further *(using her sign language)*, "We started looking for helpful and educated people in our village and came to know about a school teacher who is helpful by nature and can help us learn alphabets. We knew that we cannot complete our education, but at least we can learn how to read and write sentences which we can use to communicate with people by writing on a piece of paper. We were clear that whatever we faced and suffered in life, we would have a different life for our children and not let them suffer. Then onwards, we used to always carry a small notebook and a pen and used to write our reply to people.

As my elder son grew up, he understood our problem and the hardship we faced while dealing with the villagers. He decided to stand on his feet and make us proud and even get back the respect in society that his parents deserved. My elder son strongly faced all the torments from the village people, but he never retaliated or spoke badly to others."

It is the kind of actions you take at each stage of your life that helps you carve your destiny and change your future. But you have to be focused and self-responsible.

"After graduating from the government college, my elder son used to stand outside the coaching centre to get the practice question papers of the banking exam. When a tutor came to know about this, he used to provide him with a few sample question papers every week. My elder son practised solving those questions all by himself. He could not afford the coaching centre fee, but those question papers helped him prepare for his bank entrance exam. As he was elder, he even took the responsibility of educating his brother and sister."

(She could not stop her tears; she started weeping and went to her room)

Poorabh smiled and said, "Yeah, this way, my parents worked hard, and it was paid off when bhaiya got a job in SBI Bank at a clerical post. The news spread across the village; some were happy, some were envious, and some even suspected it was true. Because of my brother, my parents now get respect in the village, but many still mock us. We ignore them as we know that it is no use making them understand.

I have completed my graduation and currently got an accountants job in a private company. But I want to become a Cricketer. Soon I will be playing at the state level and then hope to represent Team India one day, so I am practicing hard.

My elder sister is now married, and she stays in Delhi. She is a school teacher by profession, and all this was possible because of Maa-Papa and Suraj bhaiya."

Parth and I were speechless hearing their heart-touching story.

"Hats off to you all. The way you all supported your parents and stood with them like a supporting pillar during tough times is commendable," Parth said and hugged Poorabh, giving him a pat on his back.

Only having resources does not make us capable of achieving everything in life. The most important things we need to achieve our goals are self-belief, self-discipline, and determination.

If we are strong enough and dare to face all the difficulties and challenges in life with a positive mindset, we will be successful and come out as a winner.

The Message

After having the delicious dinner, we all went to sleep.

While in bed, I was thinking that there would be many such people in this world who are suffering, but only a few dare to fight and achieve extraordinary success by defeating their problems. There are many such hidden success stories we don't even know about.

We worry too much about our problems and challenges and waste a lot of time just thinking about them.

Instead of wasting time, we can think about what action we could take to overcome those problems. Once we start doing that, we will soon be able to call ourselves successful and happy people.

Circumstances will not always favour you. What will you do then?

Will you easily give up, or will you try to find ways to overcome them?

Sometimes it is easy to say but difficult to do; still, it may not be impossible to do it.

I had learnt a big life lesson that day, and their happy faces made me realise that whatever you want in life, you can get it if you have the will and the courage!

I woke up hearing the crowing of a rooster. The digital clock on my mobile phone showed 5:00 AM.

"Get up; we need to leave and complete our journey," I whispered slowly to Parth.

"Yeah, we will not wake them up; otherwise, their sleep will get disturbed," replied Parth.

We wrote a note and kept it on the dressing table...

"We are leaving, and we don't want you all to get disturbed. Thank you for the lovely and memorable time.

We will visit again soon. Take care and lots of love.

- Parth & Kiran"

"Walk slowly!" I told Parth.

"Oh, No! We need a key as the gate is locked. We will have to wake up Poorabh," Parth said.

(Parth slowly entered his room) "Poorabh! Poorabh! Please get up."

"You both are going; it's too early," Poorabh responded, rubbing his eyes while still half-sleep.

"Yes, we need to complete our journey," replied Parth.

Meanwhile, his parents too, were awake.

Her mother gave me a small box containing vermillion and a dozen red glass bangles.

She kissed me on my forehead, and with moist eyes, she bid me and Parth farewell and showered her blessings on us.

Poorabh's father made some sign language and told us to go safely and inform us once you reach your destination.

On the way, I was just remembering about their life and understood that "Life is not always easy; there will always be some challenges in front of us. It is all about our willpower and how we plan to deal with those challenges. Moreover, we don't need words or a language to express ourselves and share our emotions, and where love dwells, language is secondary."

About The Author

Bina Roy

Bina Roy was born in Siliguri Darjeeling, West Bengal, and completed her education in this beautiful mountain city. She is an English teacher by profession and has a decade of teaching experience in various public schools.

Apart from this, she is also a certified IELTS trainer, Business Communication Coach, Writer, Editor, Content Creator, and student of public speaking. She holds a B.A. English (Hons.), M.A., B.Ed., and D.led in English.

Bina teaches IELTS students and helps them to crack IELTS. She is also a content editor for a reputed personal finance website and has also learnt mind mapping which she uses in her work life. Bina loves to read books and believes in updating one's knowledge. Since the age of 13, she has wanted to become a public speaker and influencer.

"The Gleaming Darkness" is her first book where she has scripted the ill effects of demotivation and discouragement and shows us how to overcome them.

Facing all hardships in life, she is an independent woman. She has faced many challenges in her life but stood firm in every situation with hope, courage, and a positive mindset.

Bina loves to motivate people who are suffering in their lives and believes that you can only grow if you help others grow and succeed in life. She is a lifelong learner and has a soft corner for poor and needy people.

She believes that 'to be successful in life we should keep trying, no matter whatsoever the situation may be.'

9 79888 6062786